THE GREY FAIRY BOOK

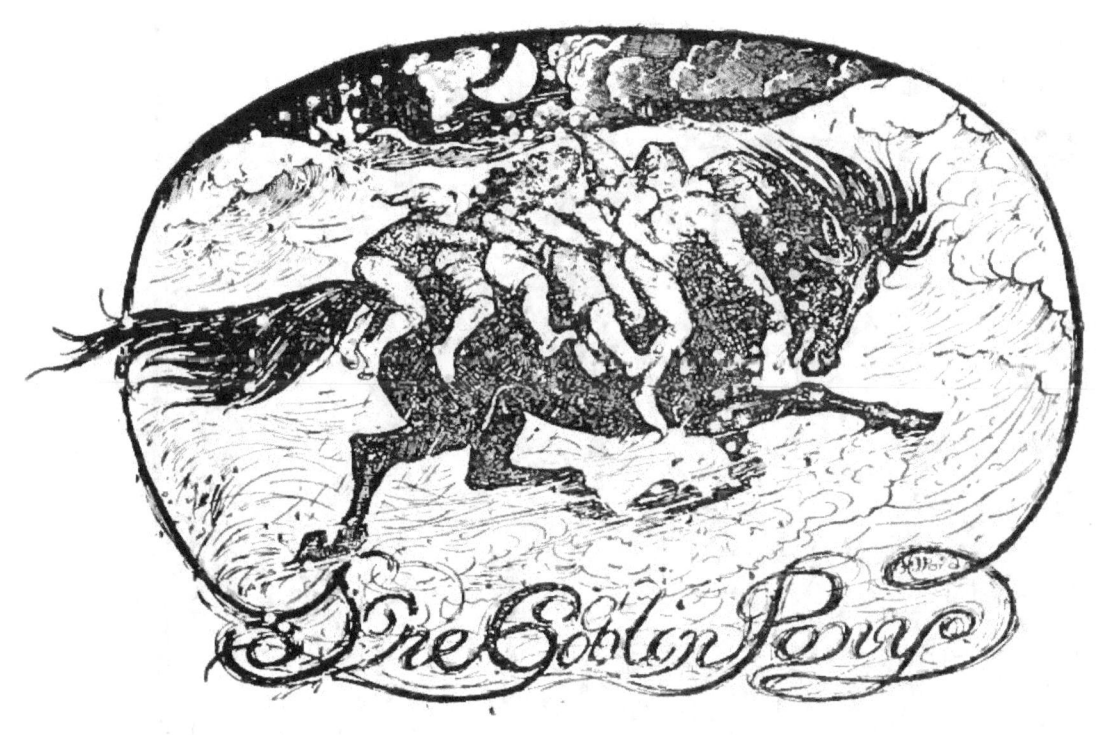

The Goblin Pony

WITH NUMEROUS ILLUSTRATIONS BY H. J. FORD

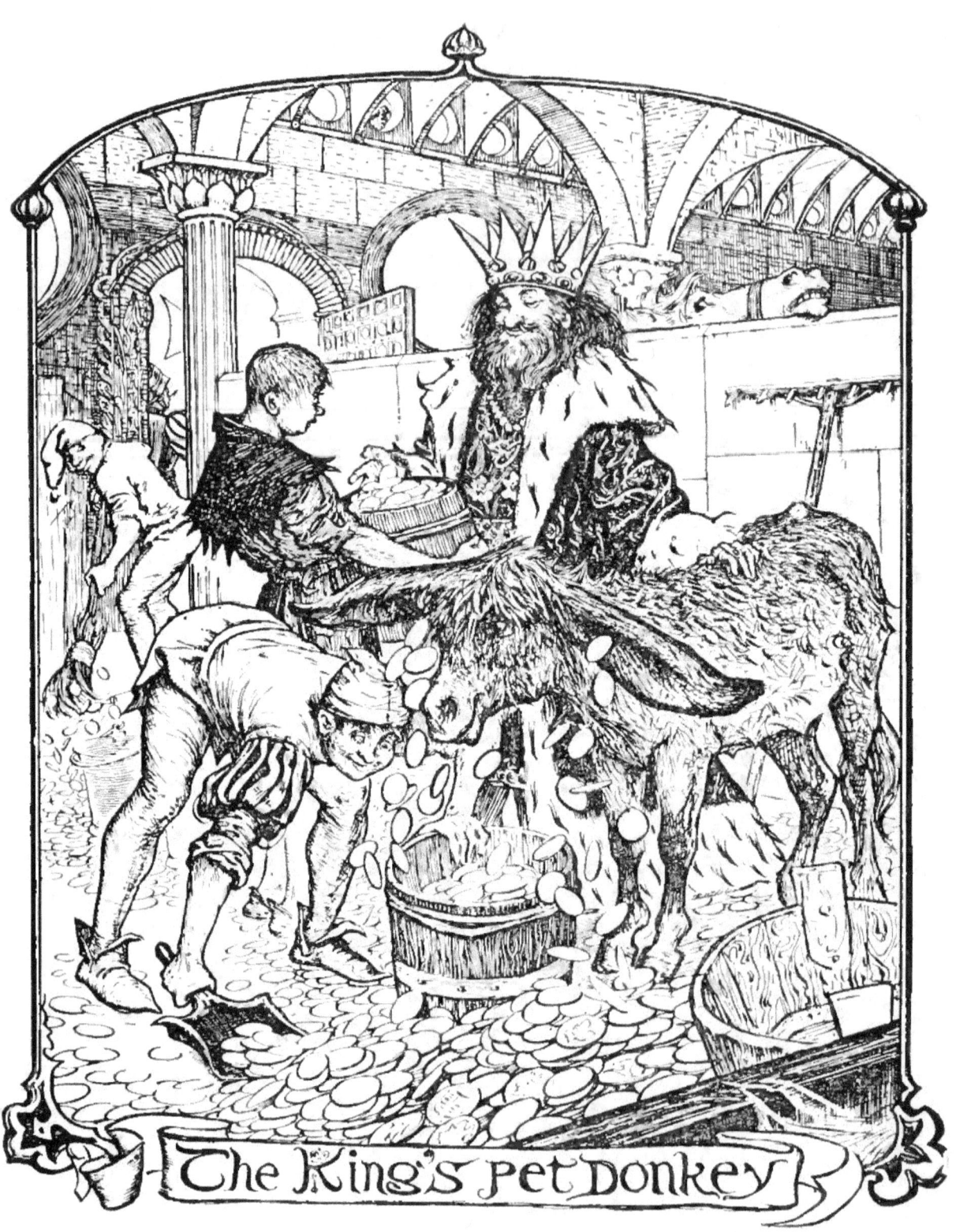

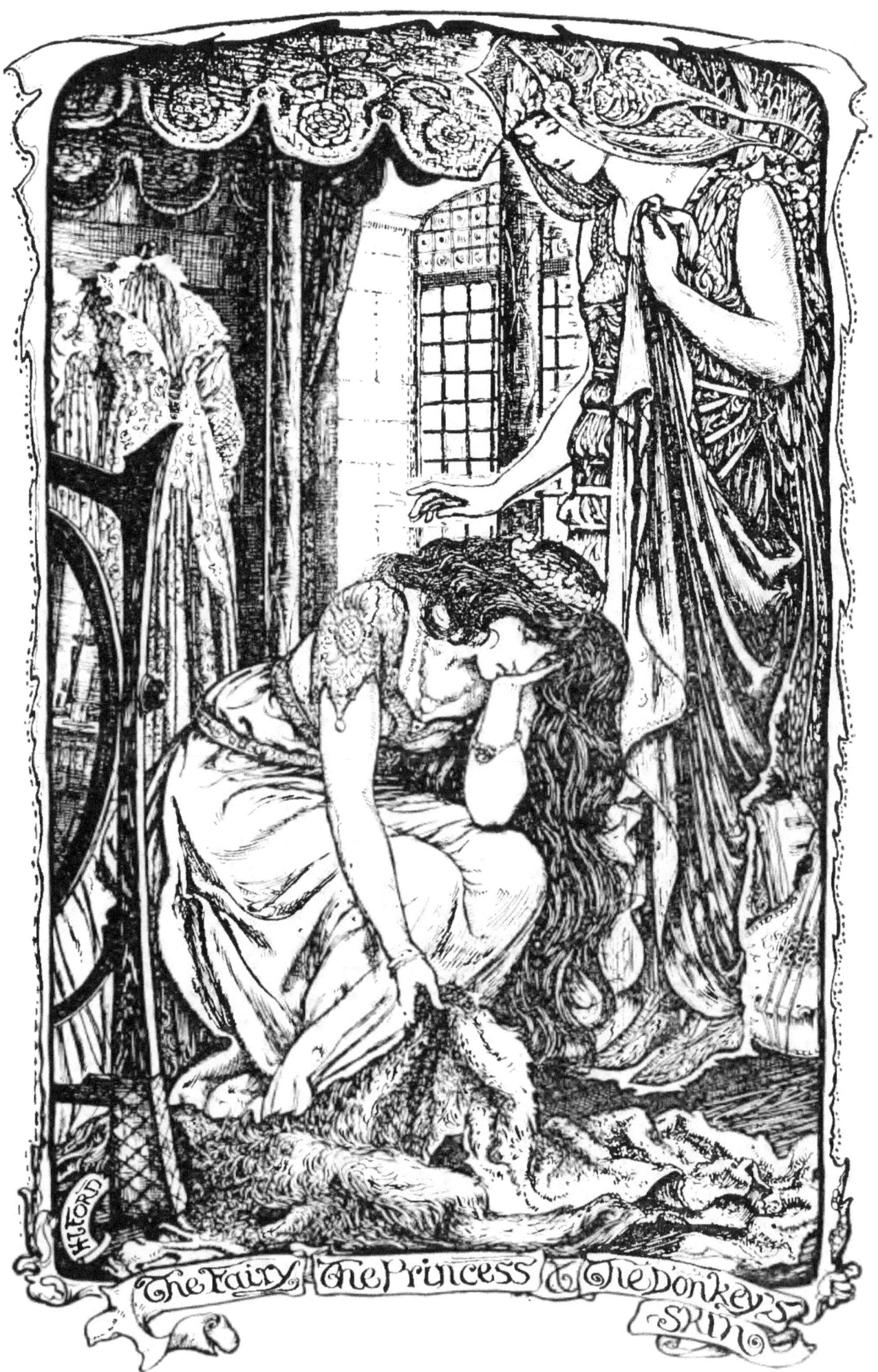

The Fairy, the Princess & the Donkey's Skin

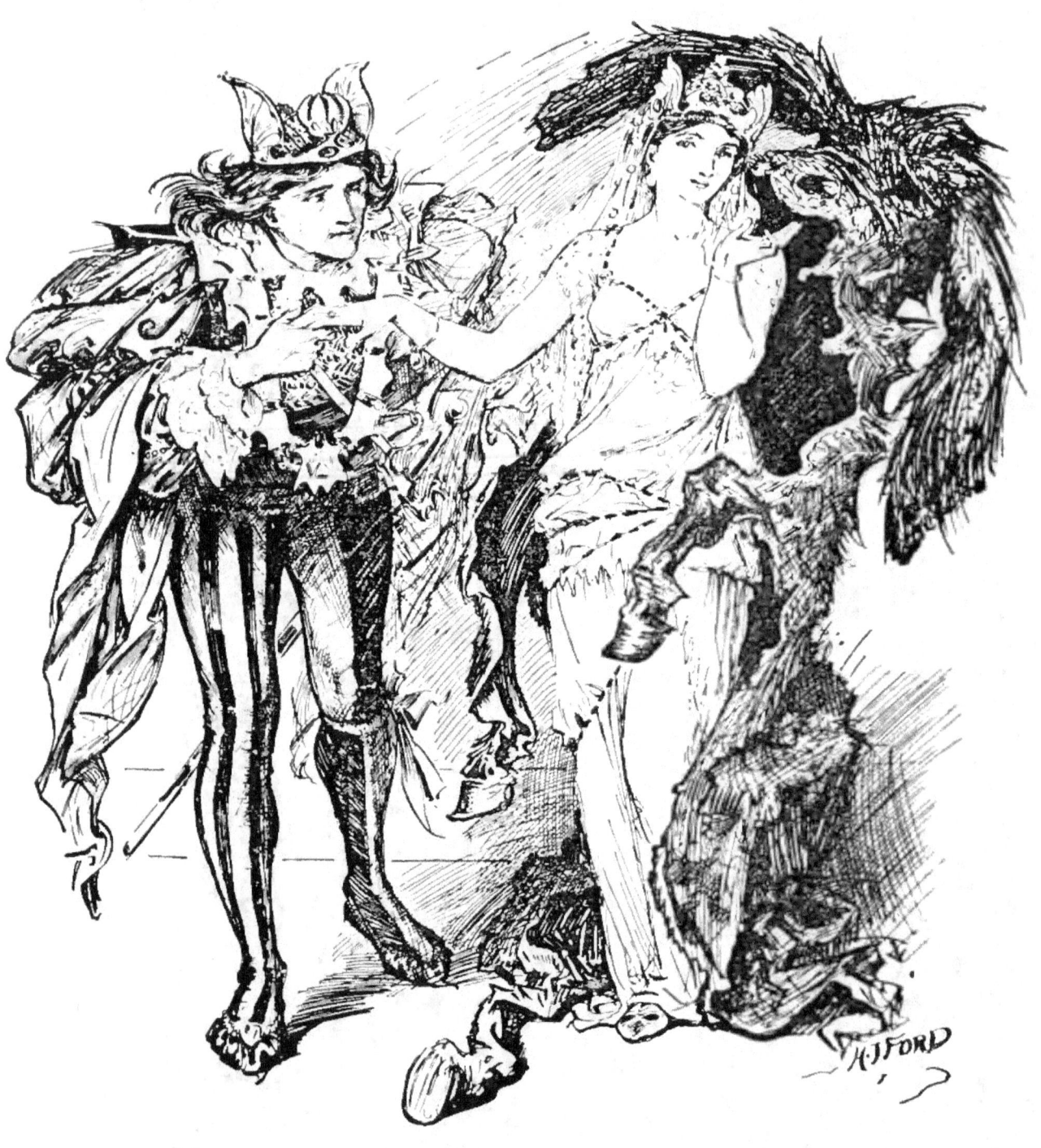

The Donkey-skin falls off.

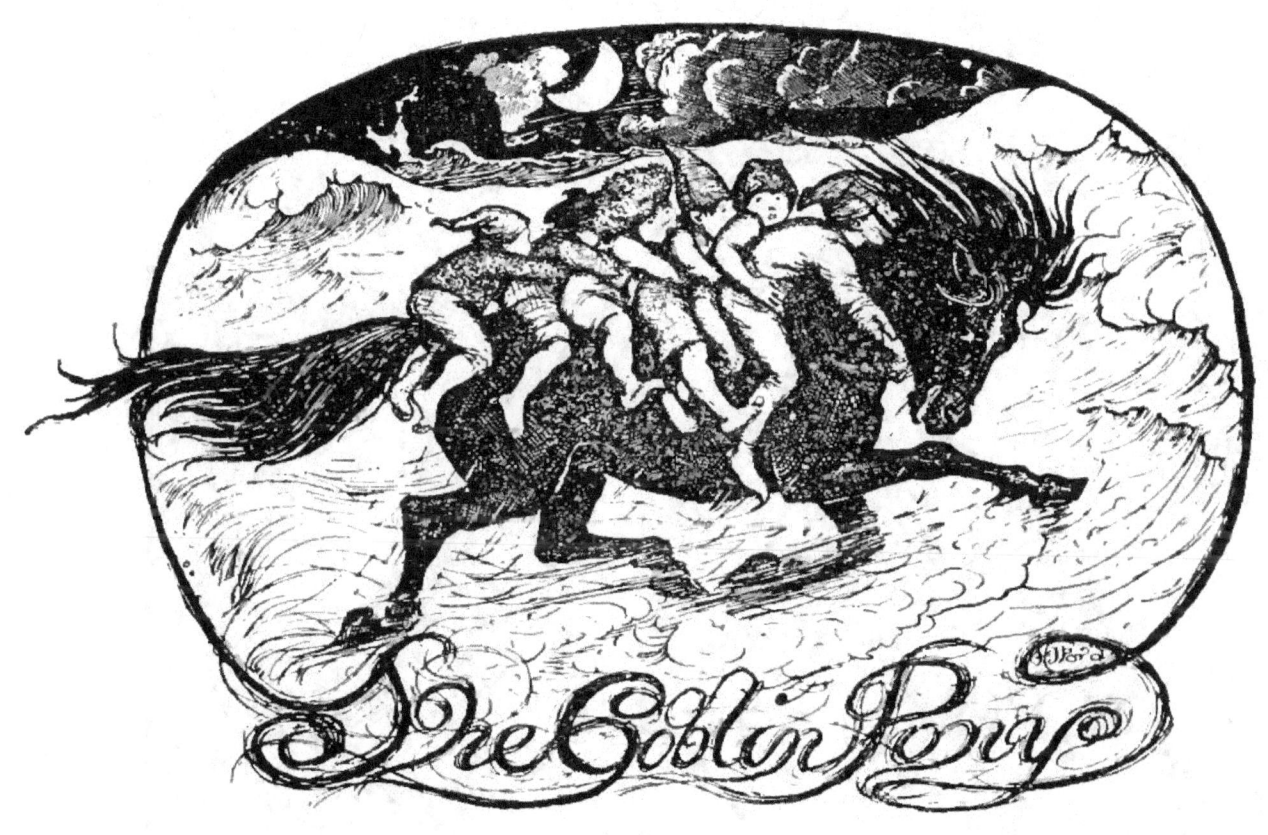

The Goblin Pony

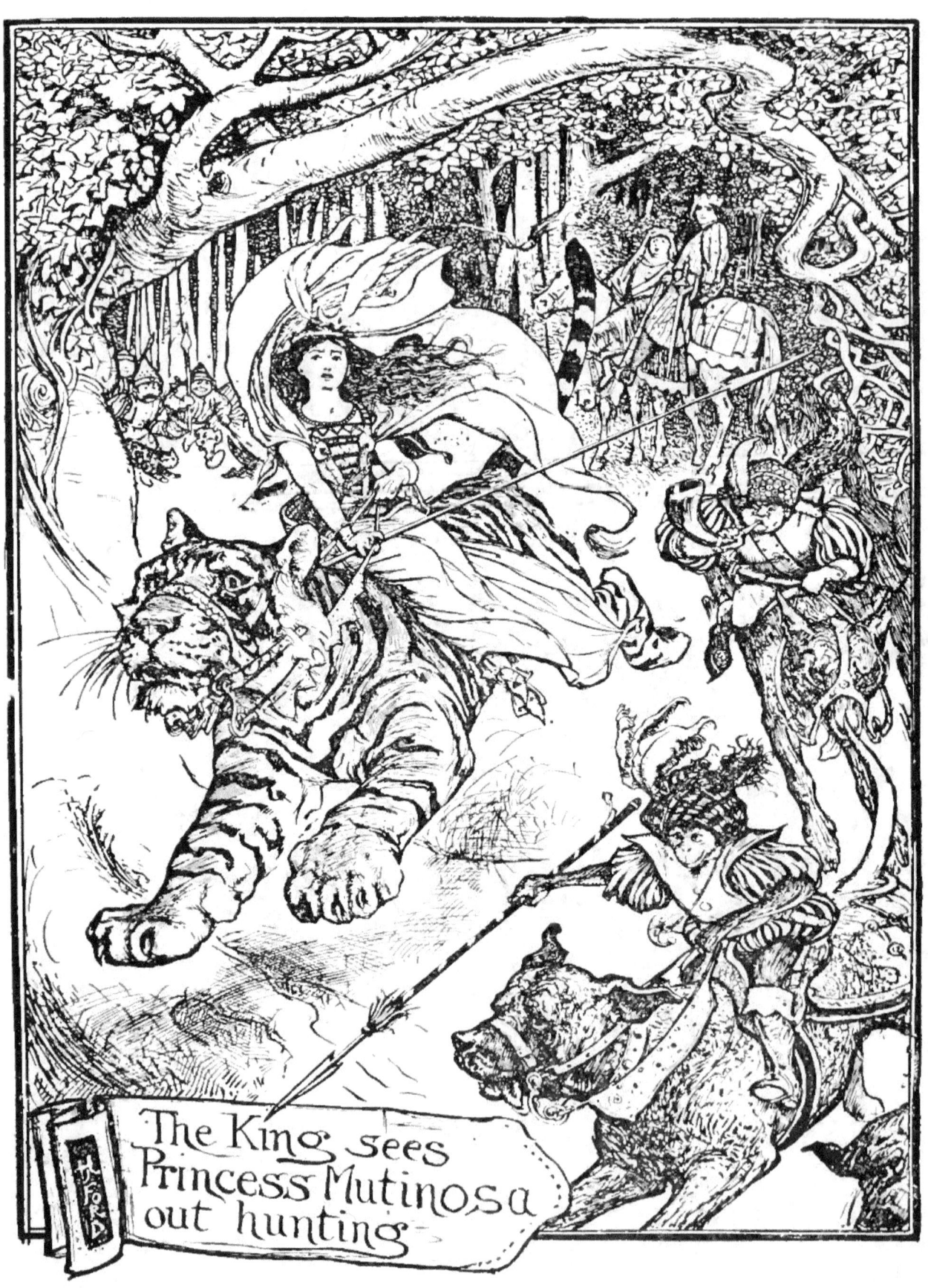

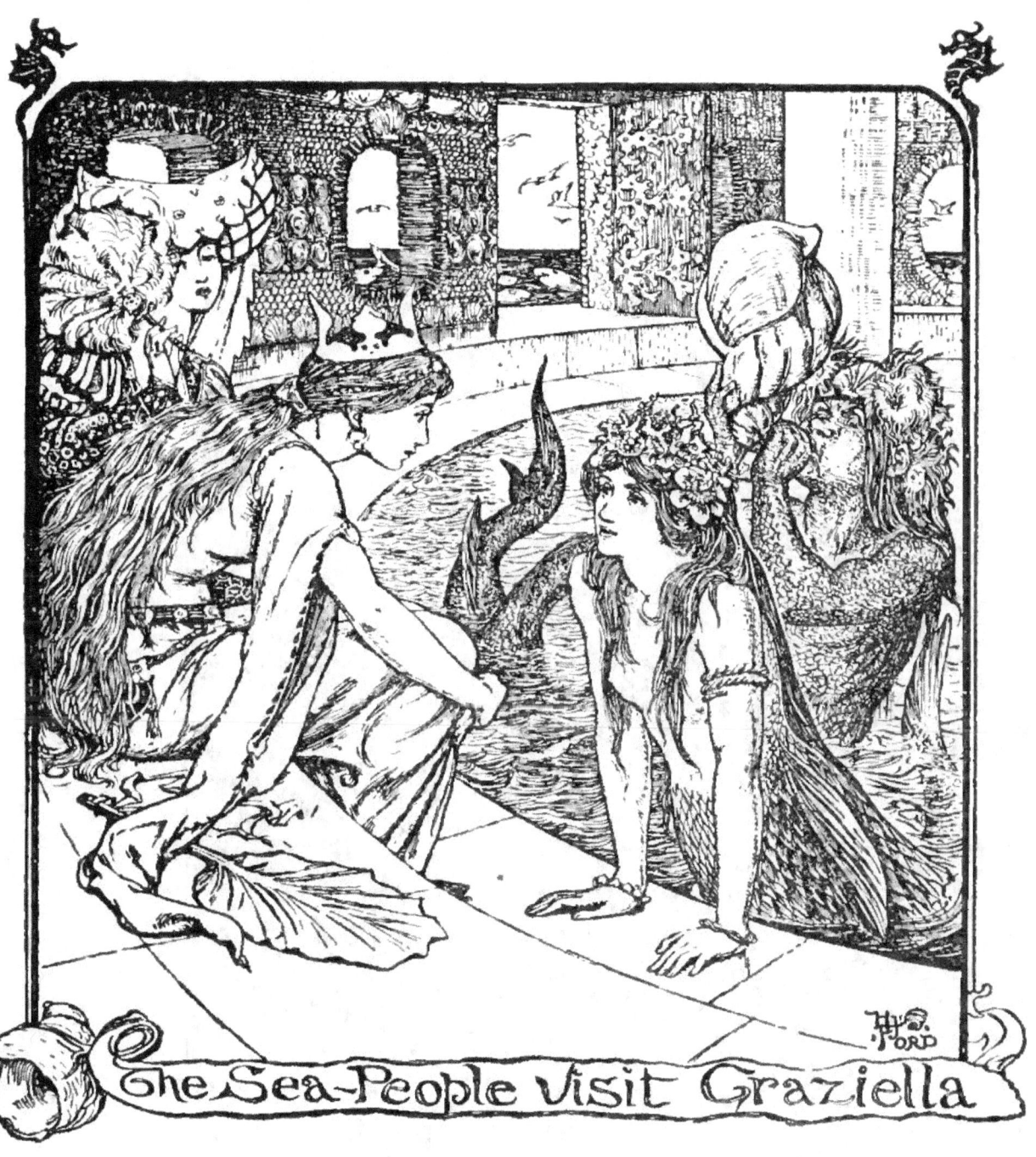

The Sea-People visit Graziella

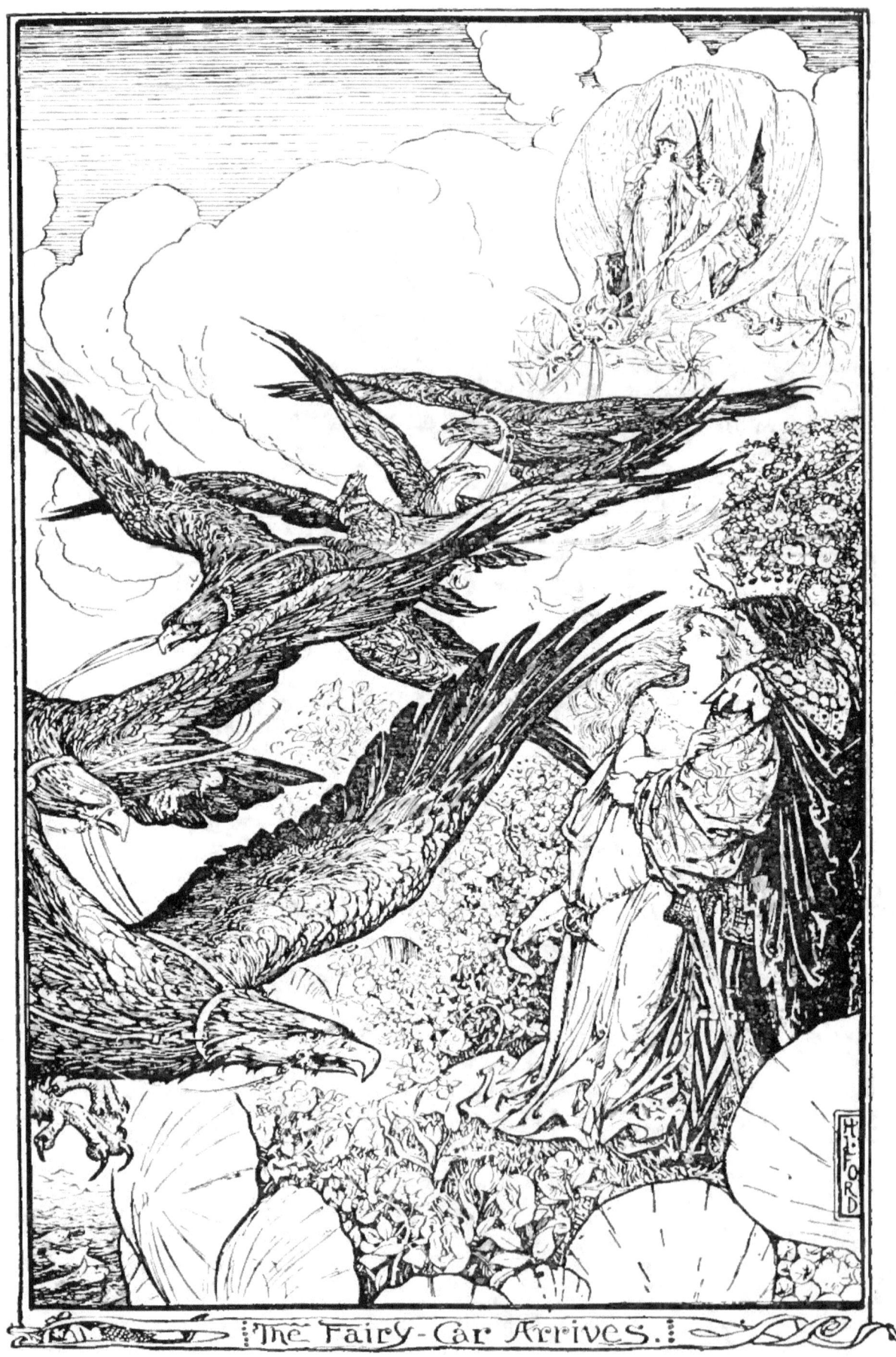

The Fairy-Car Arrives.

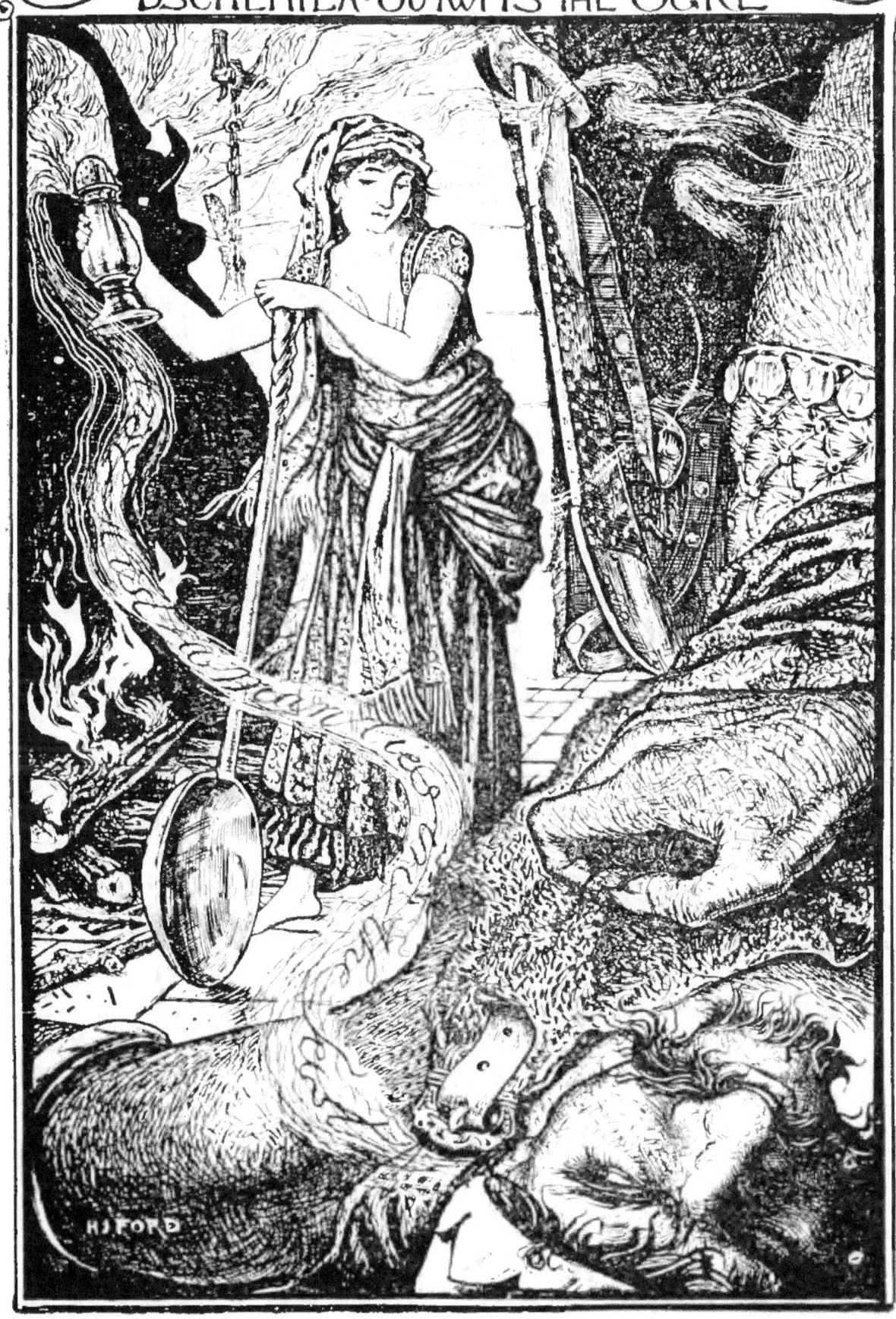

DSCHEMILA OUTWITS THE OGRE

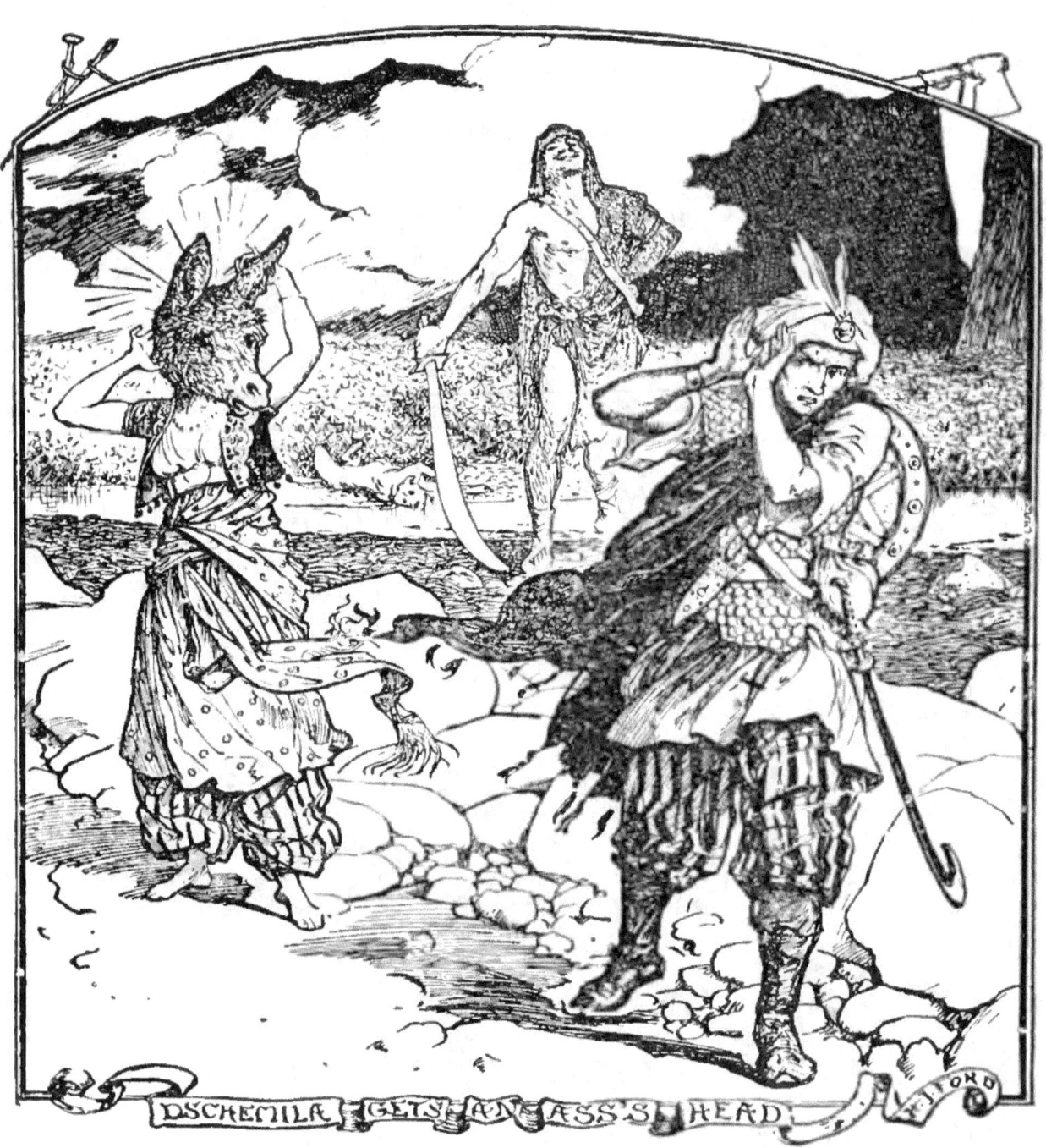
DSCHEMIL GETS AN ASS'S HEAD

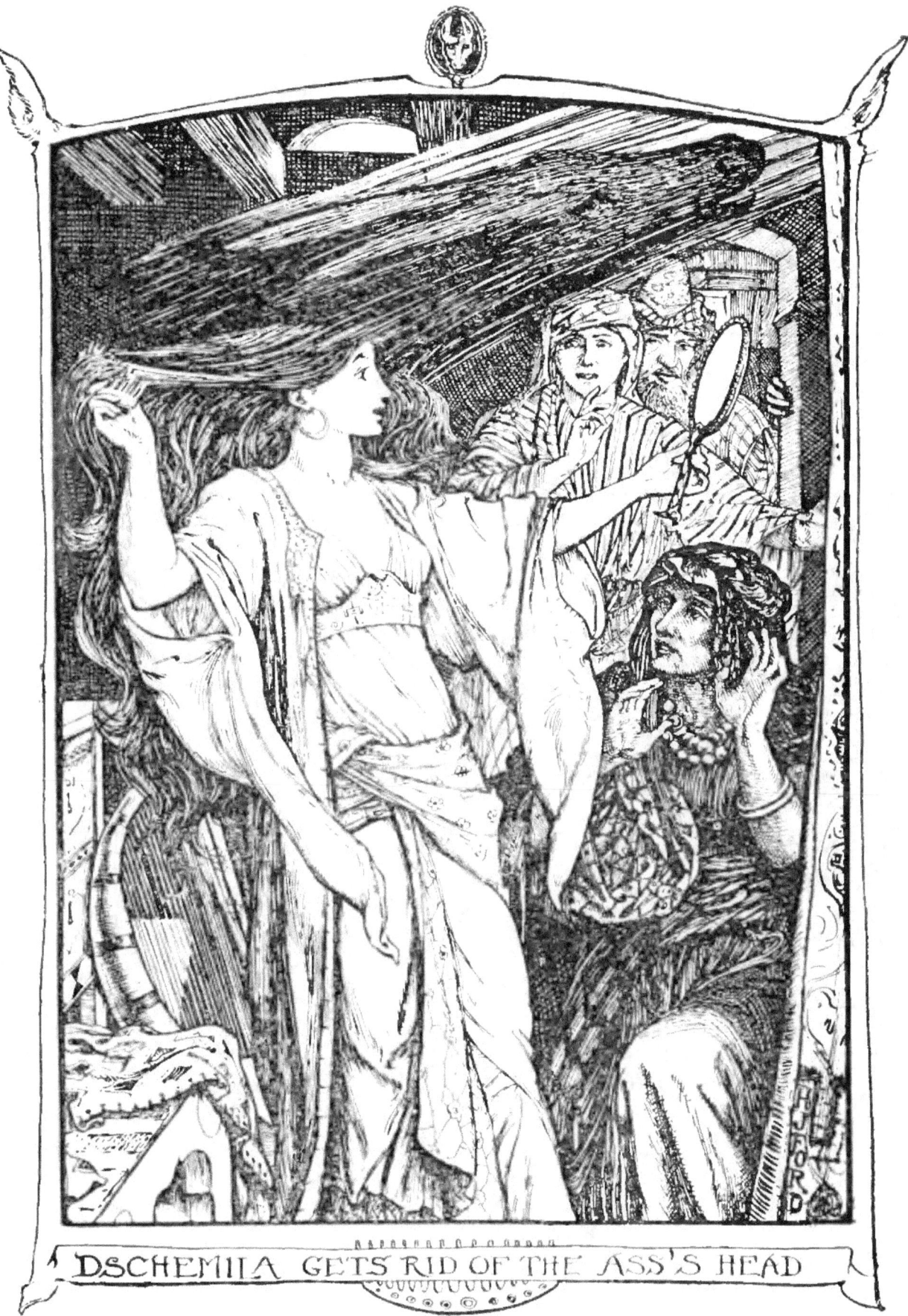
DSCHEMIIA GETS RID OF THE ASS'S HEAD

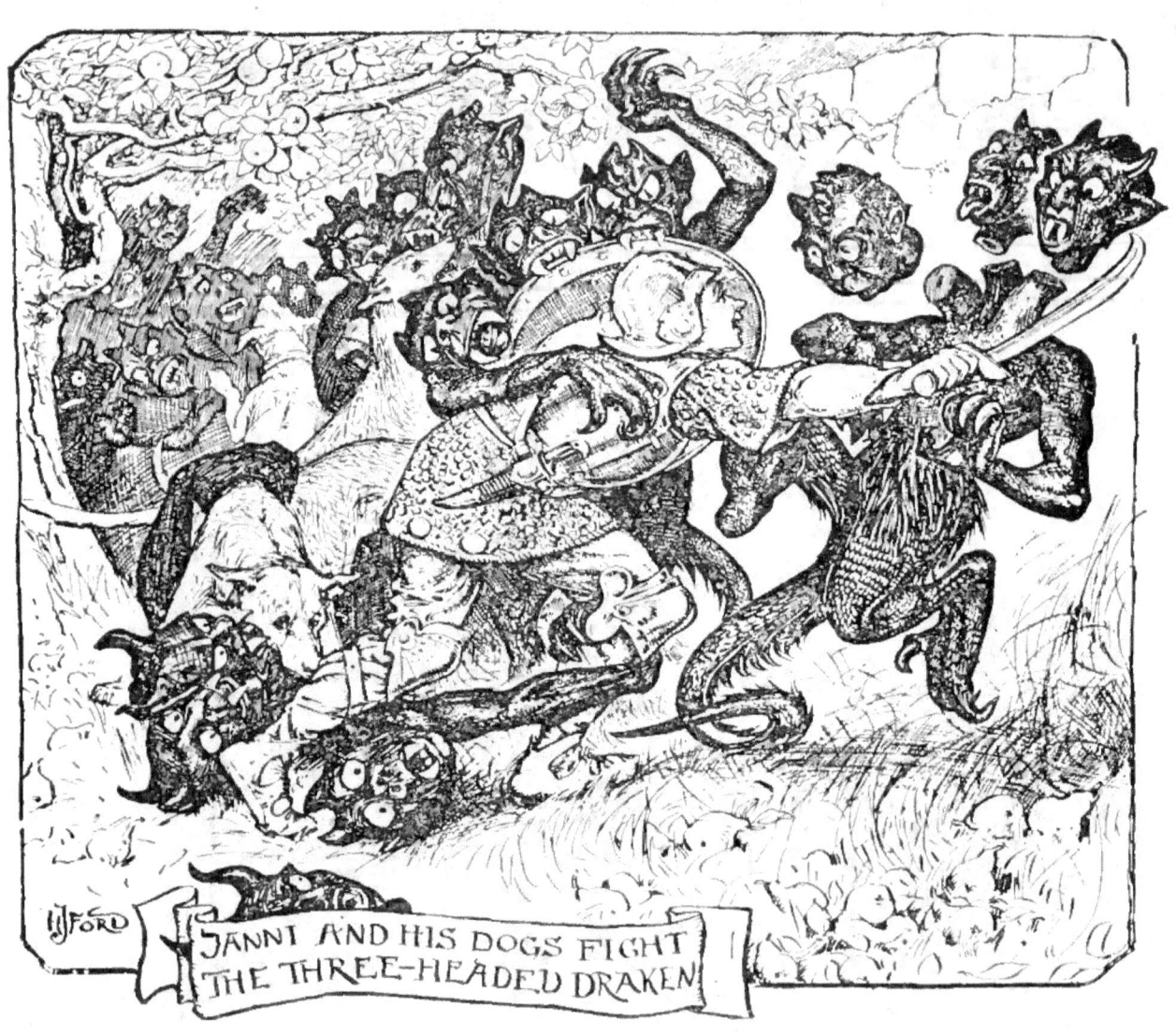

JANNI AND HIS DOGS FIGHT THE THREE-HEADED DRAKEN

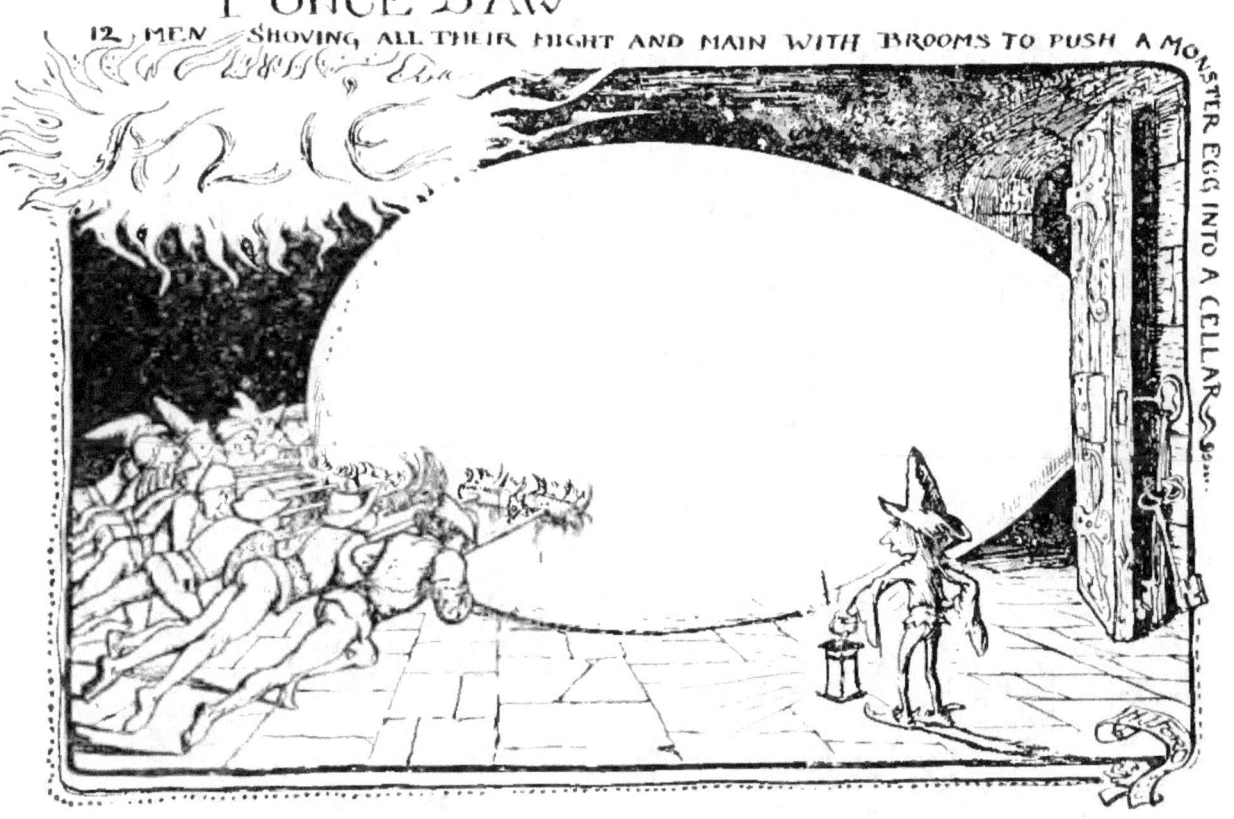

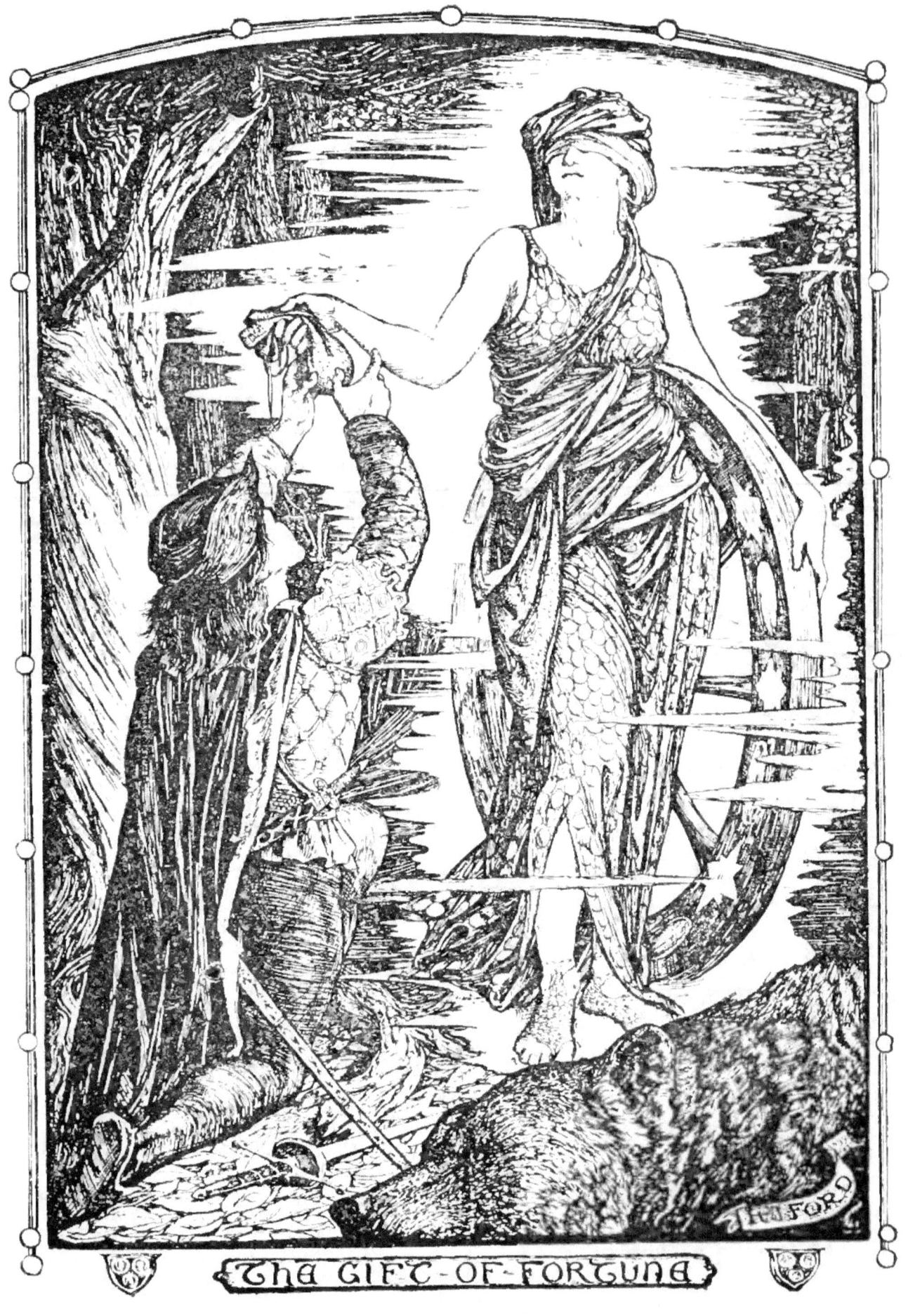
THE GIFT OF FORTUNE

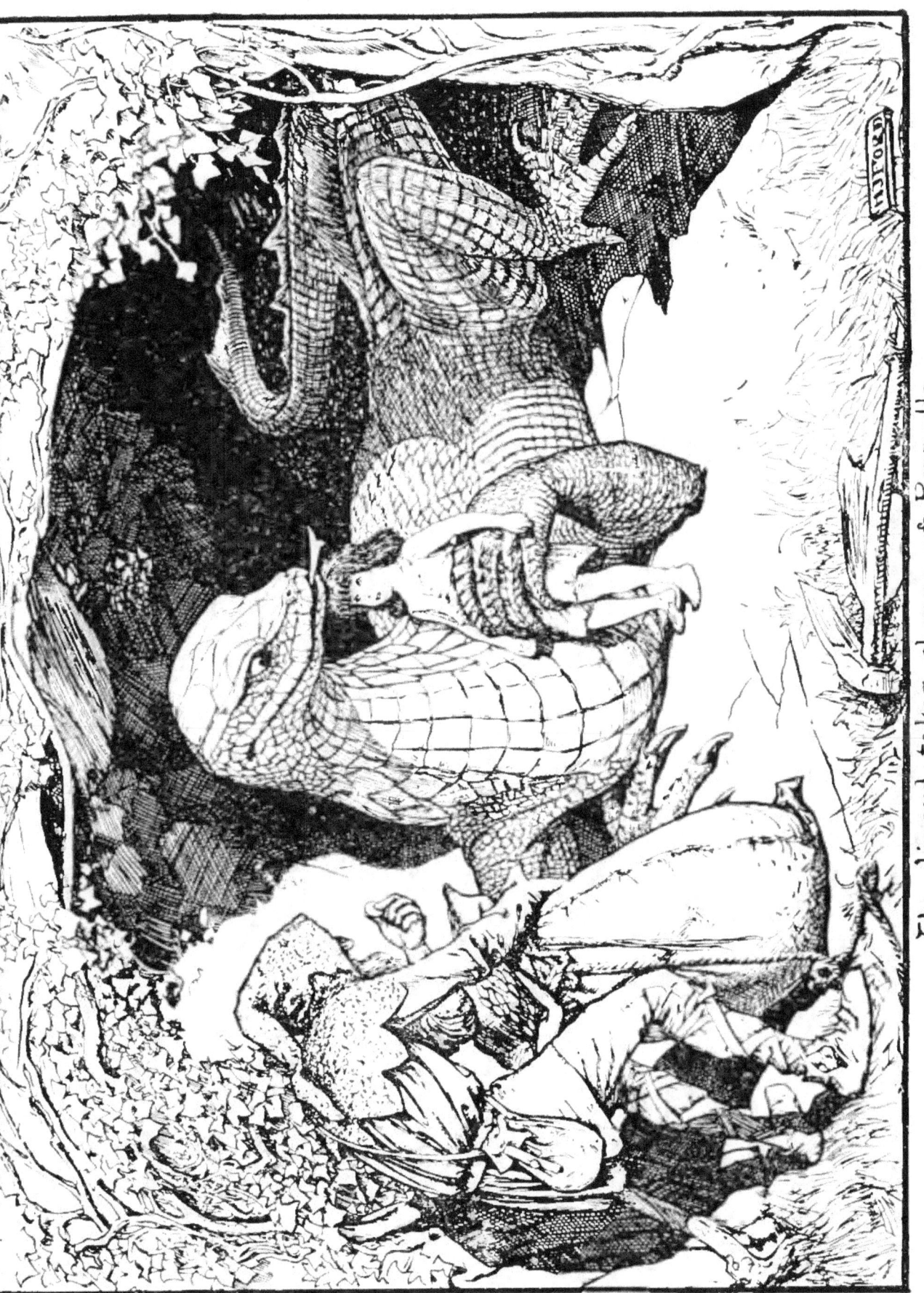

The Lizard takes charge of Renzolla

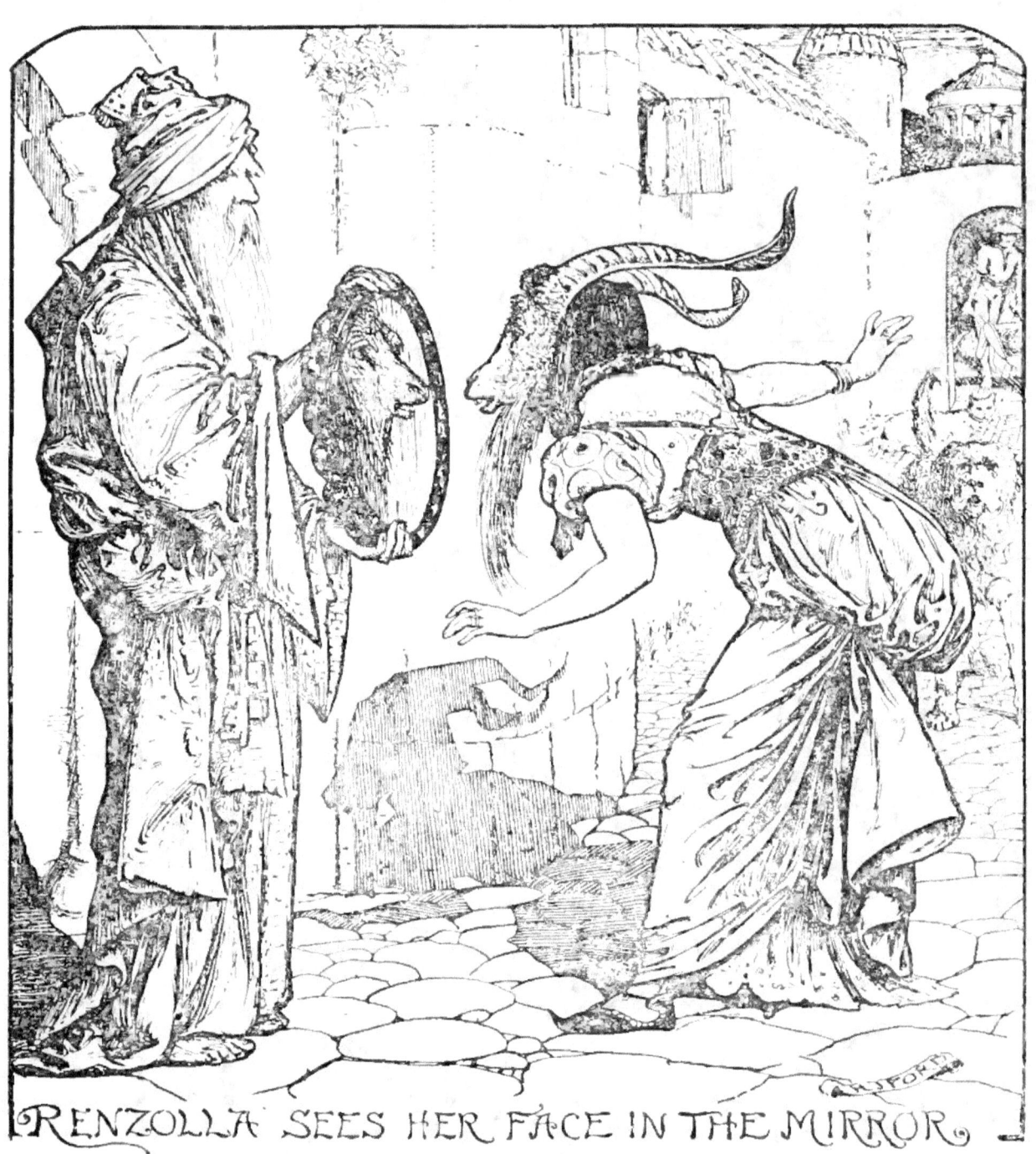
RENZOLLA SEES HER FACE IN THE MIRROR

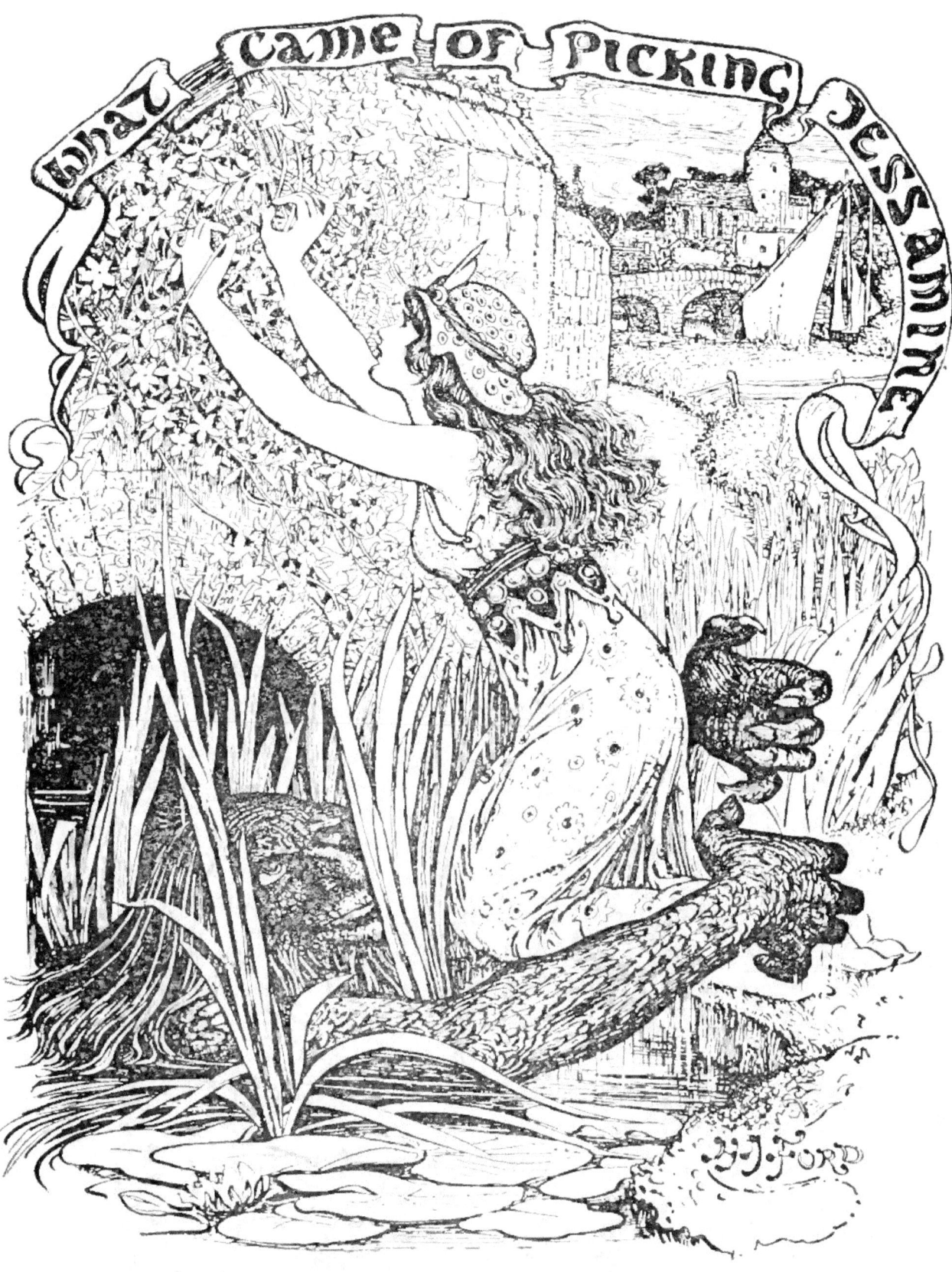

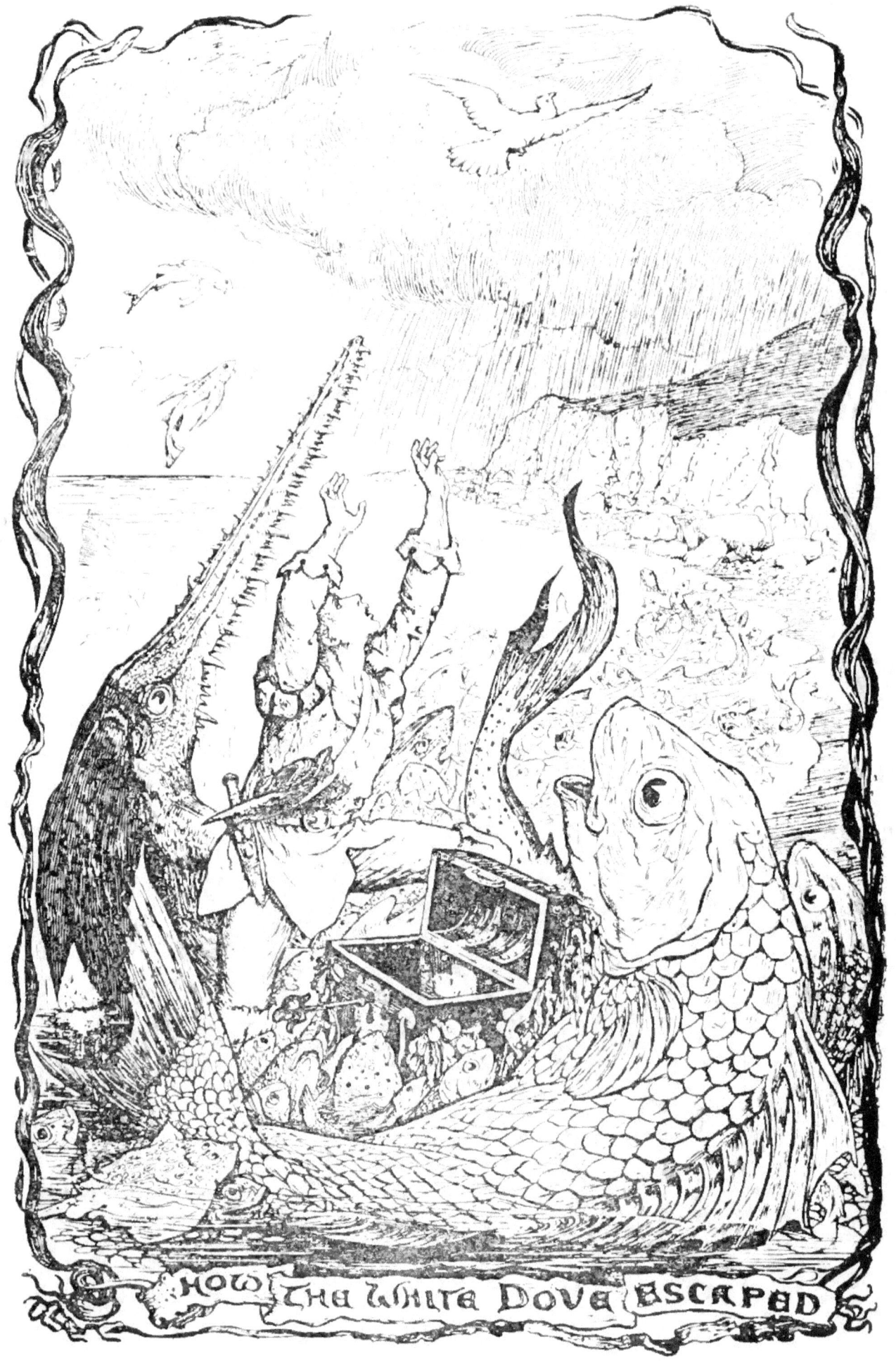
HOW THE WHITE DOVE ESCAPED

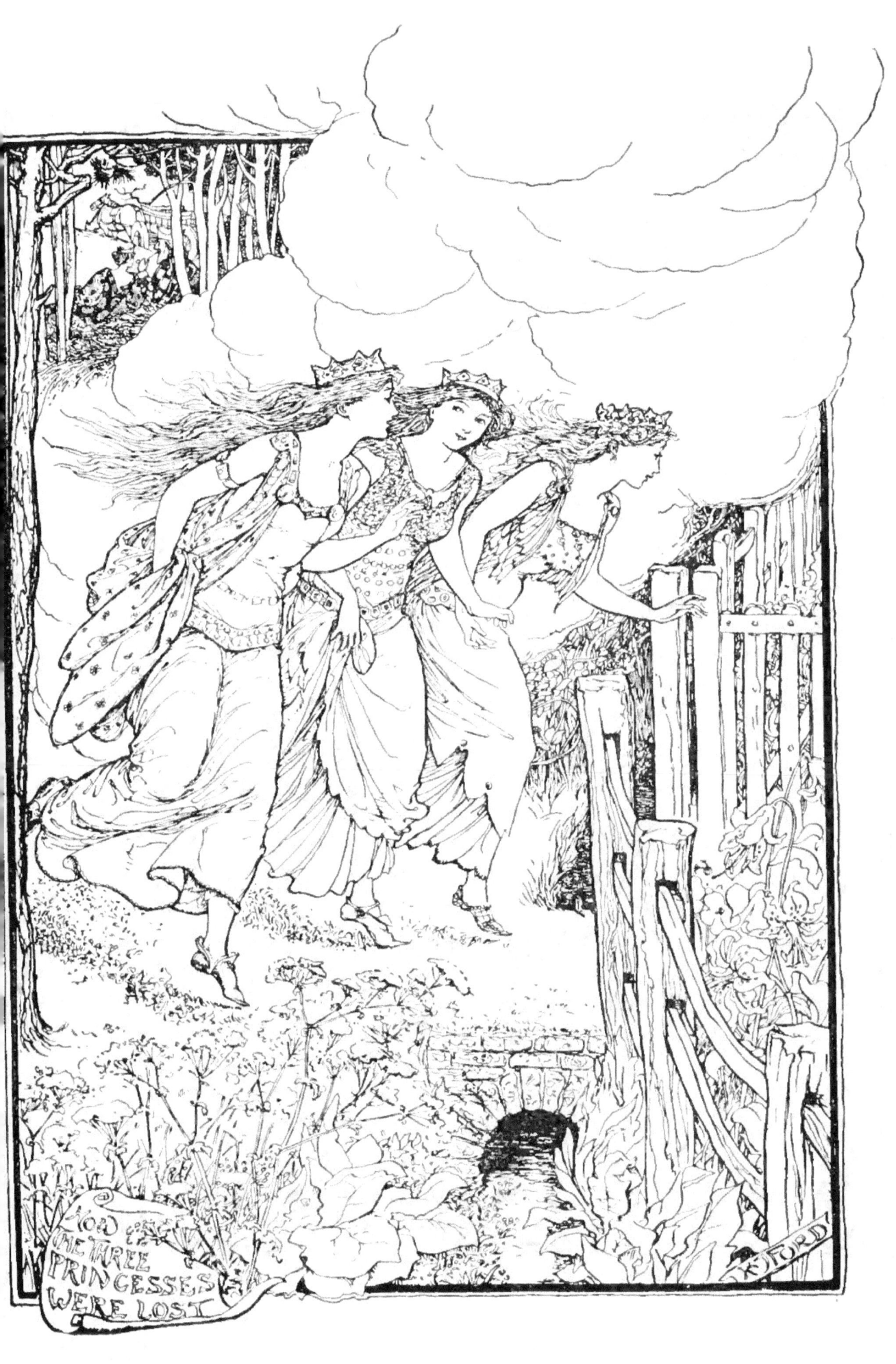

HOW THE THREE PRINCESSES WERE LOST

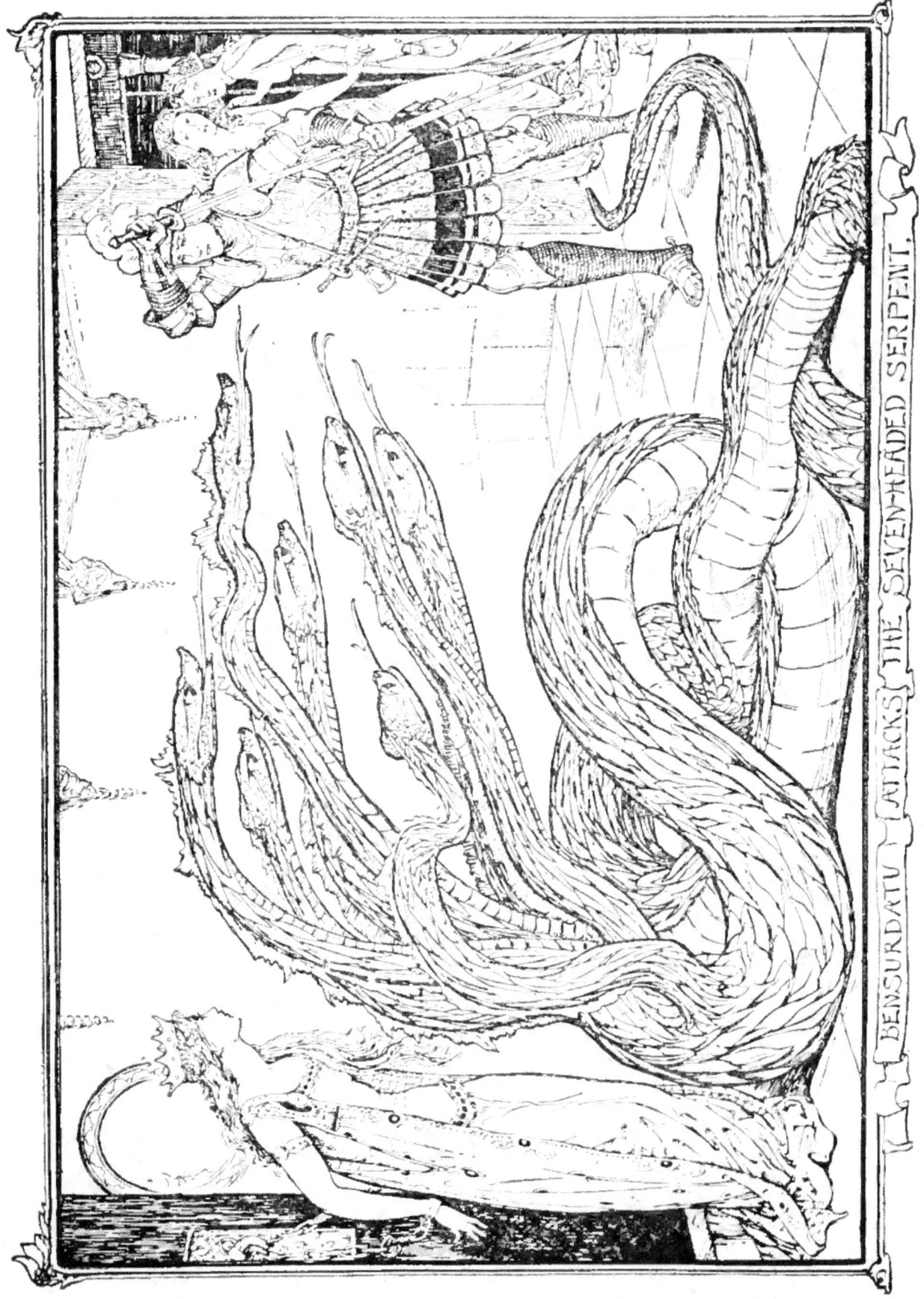
BENSURDATU ATTACKS THE SEVEN-HEADED SERPENT.

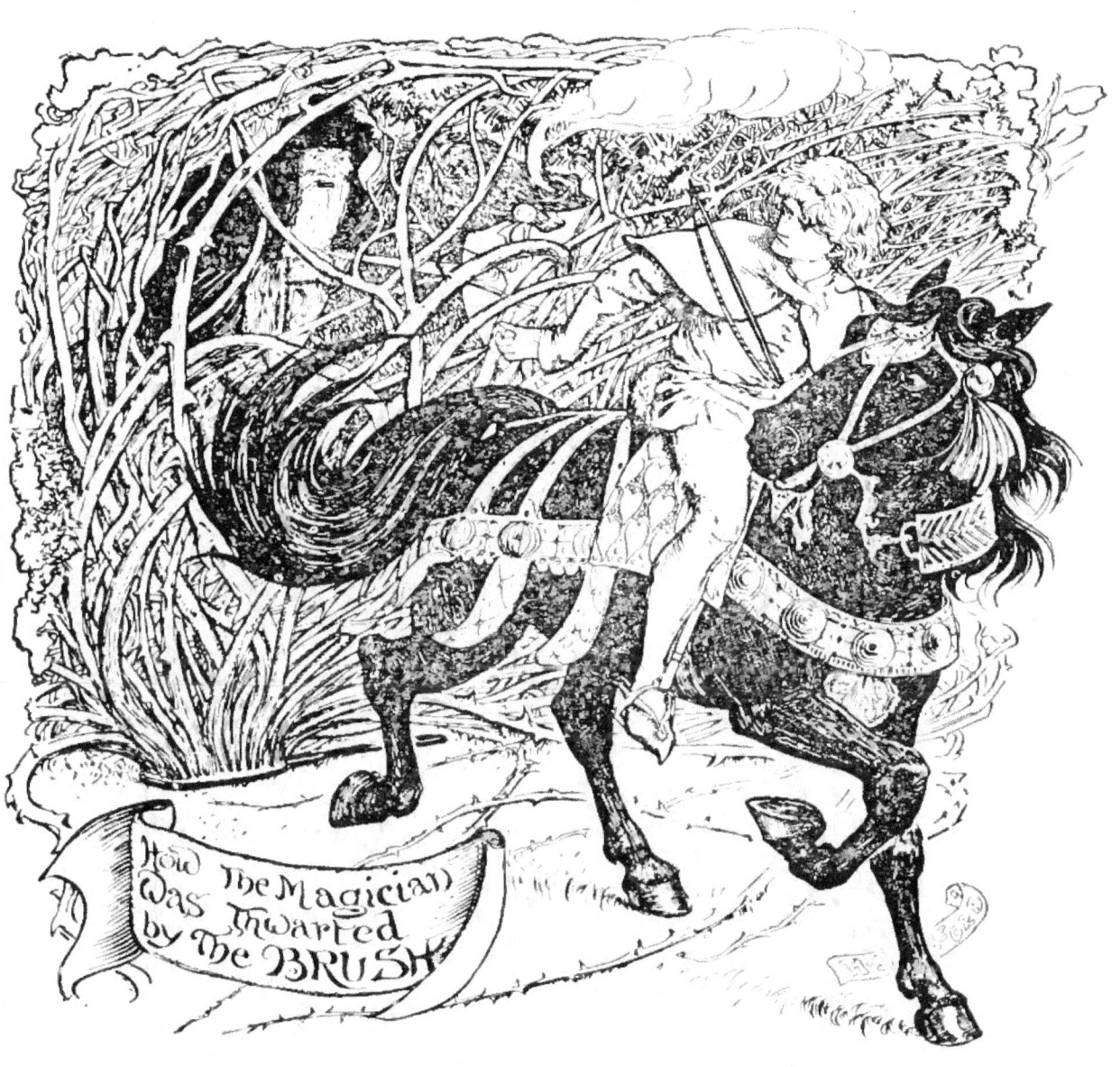

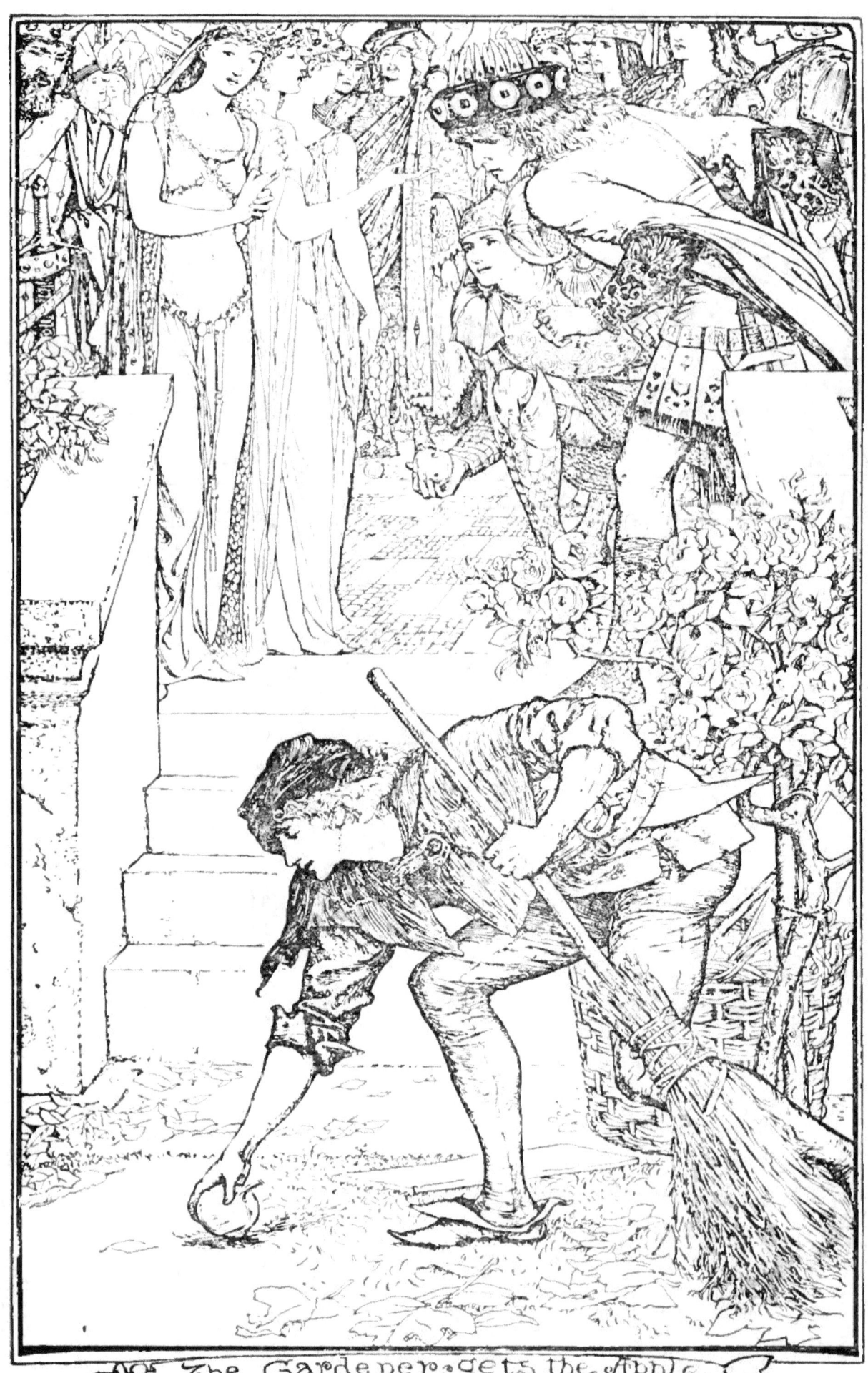
The Gardener gets the Apple

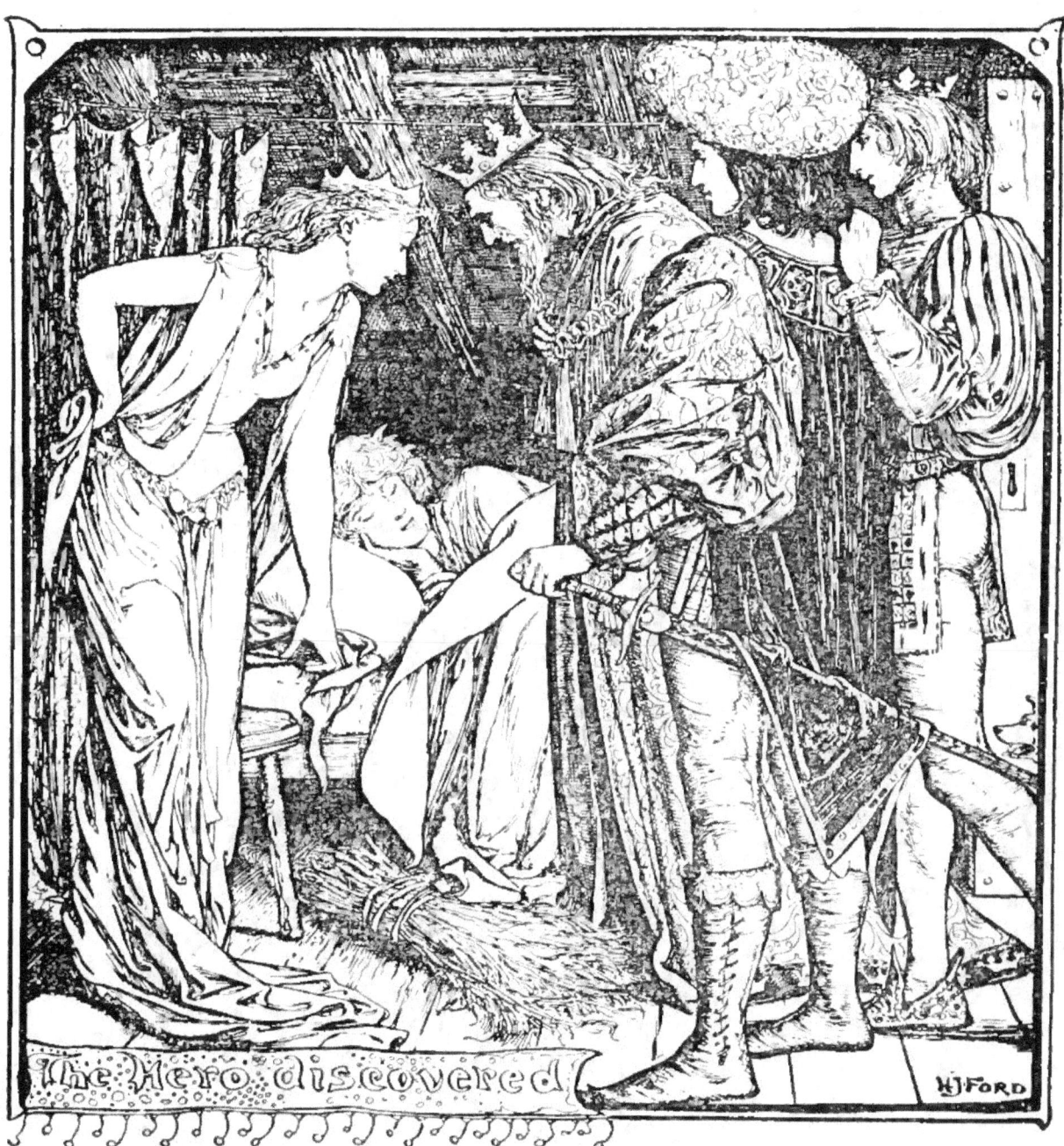

The Hero discovered

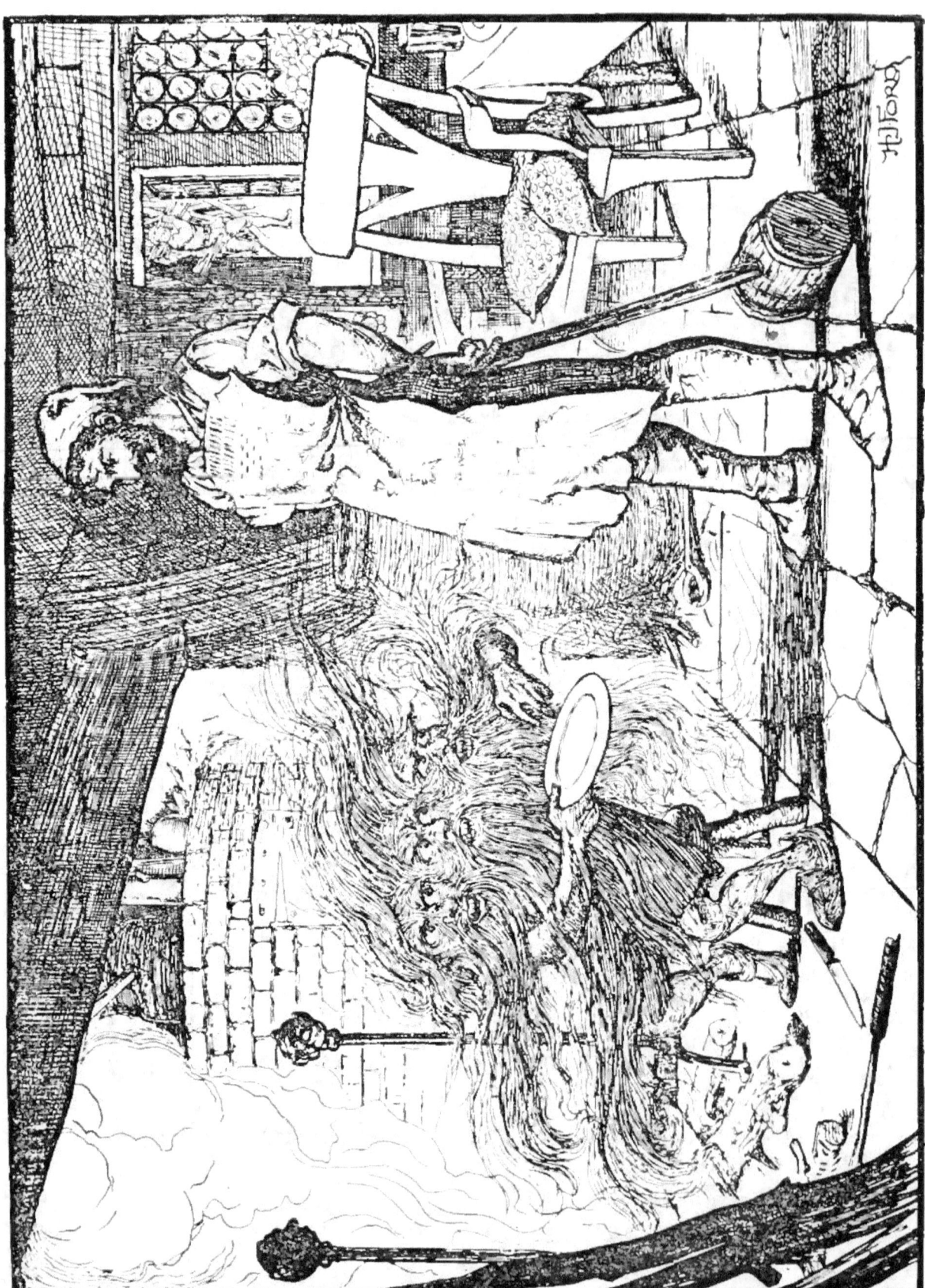

THE LITTLE GRAY MAN   "HE DEMANDED MORE"

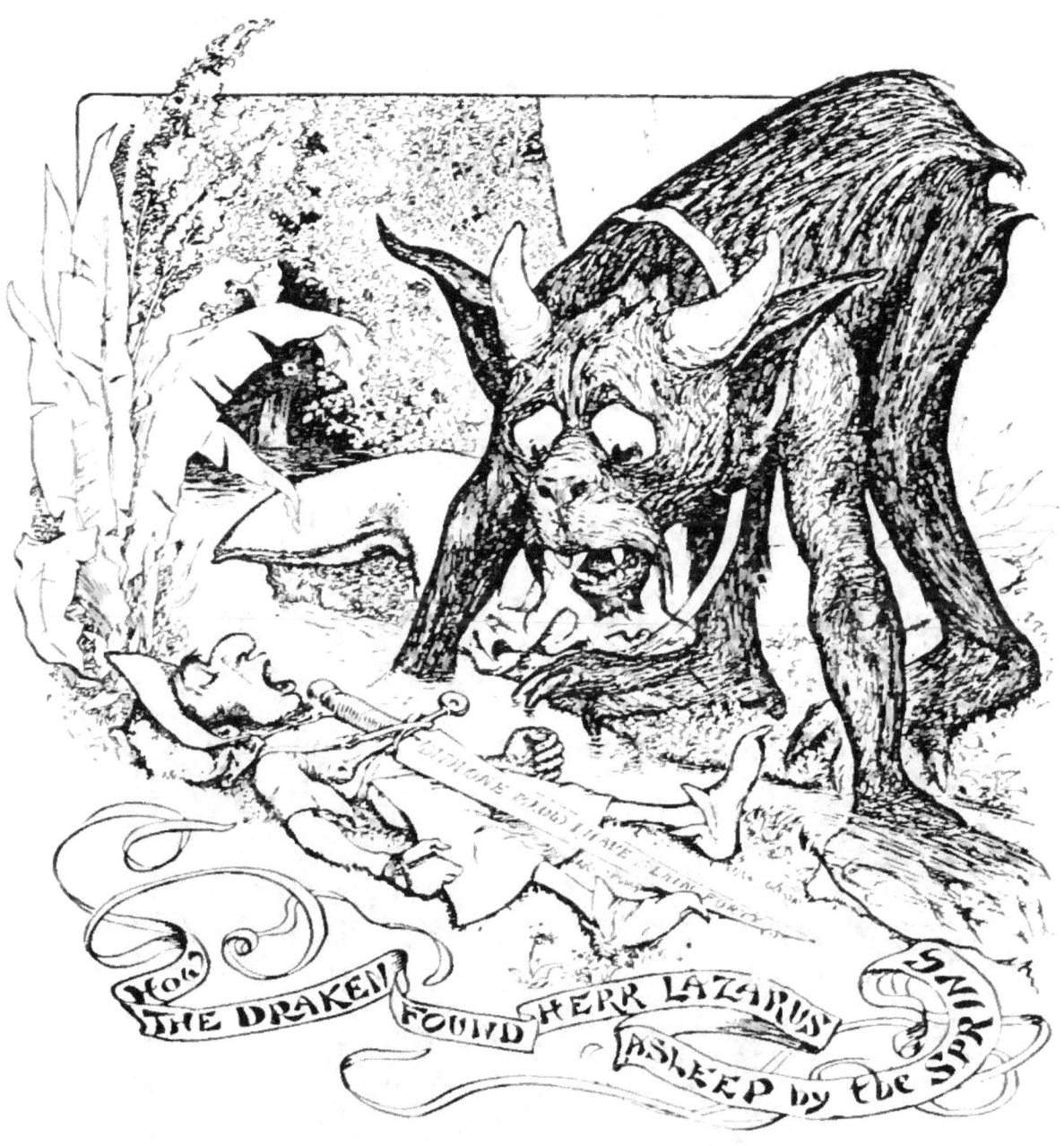

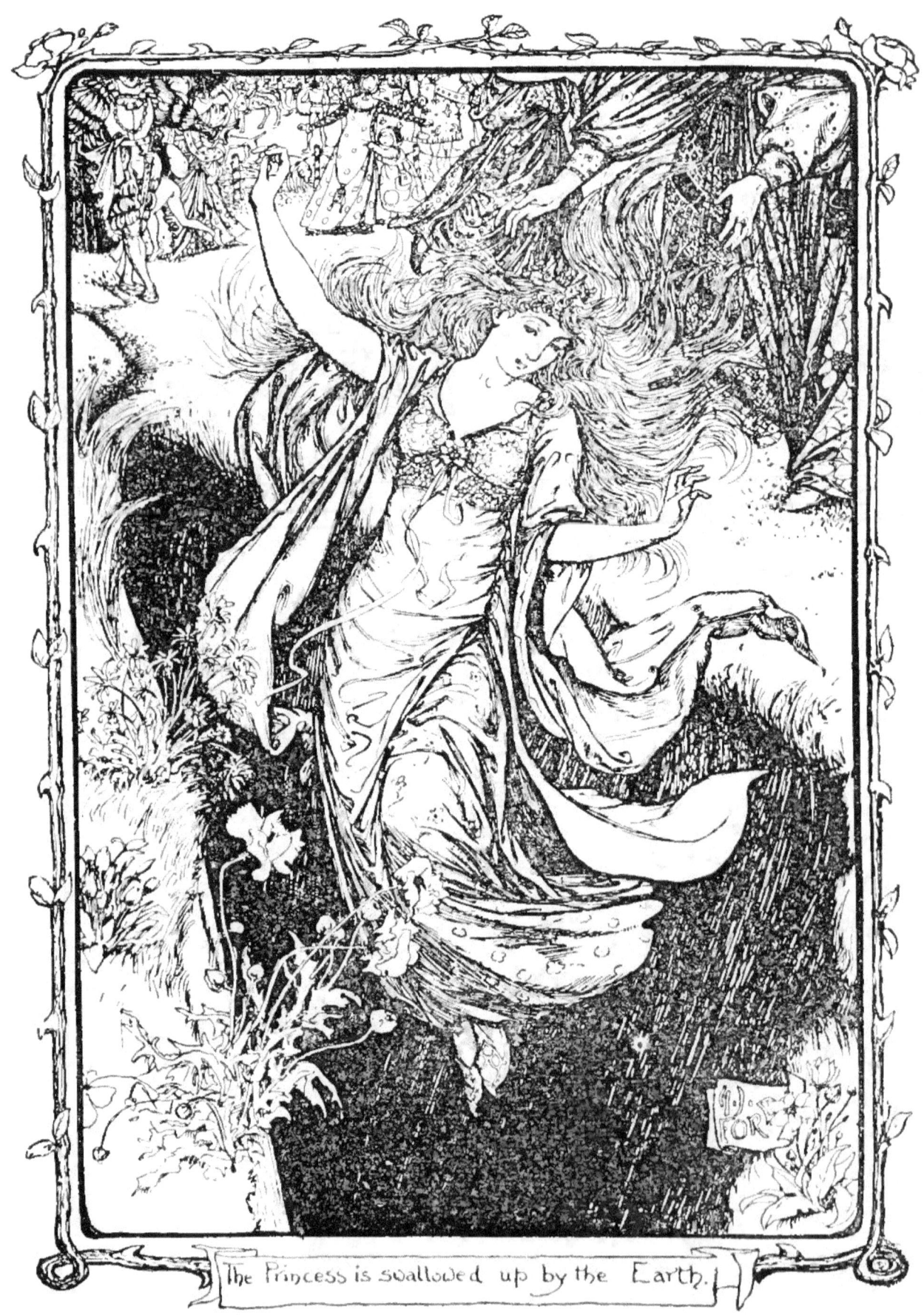

The Princess is swallowed up by the Earth.

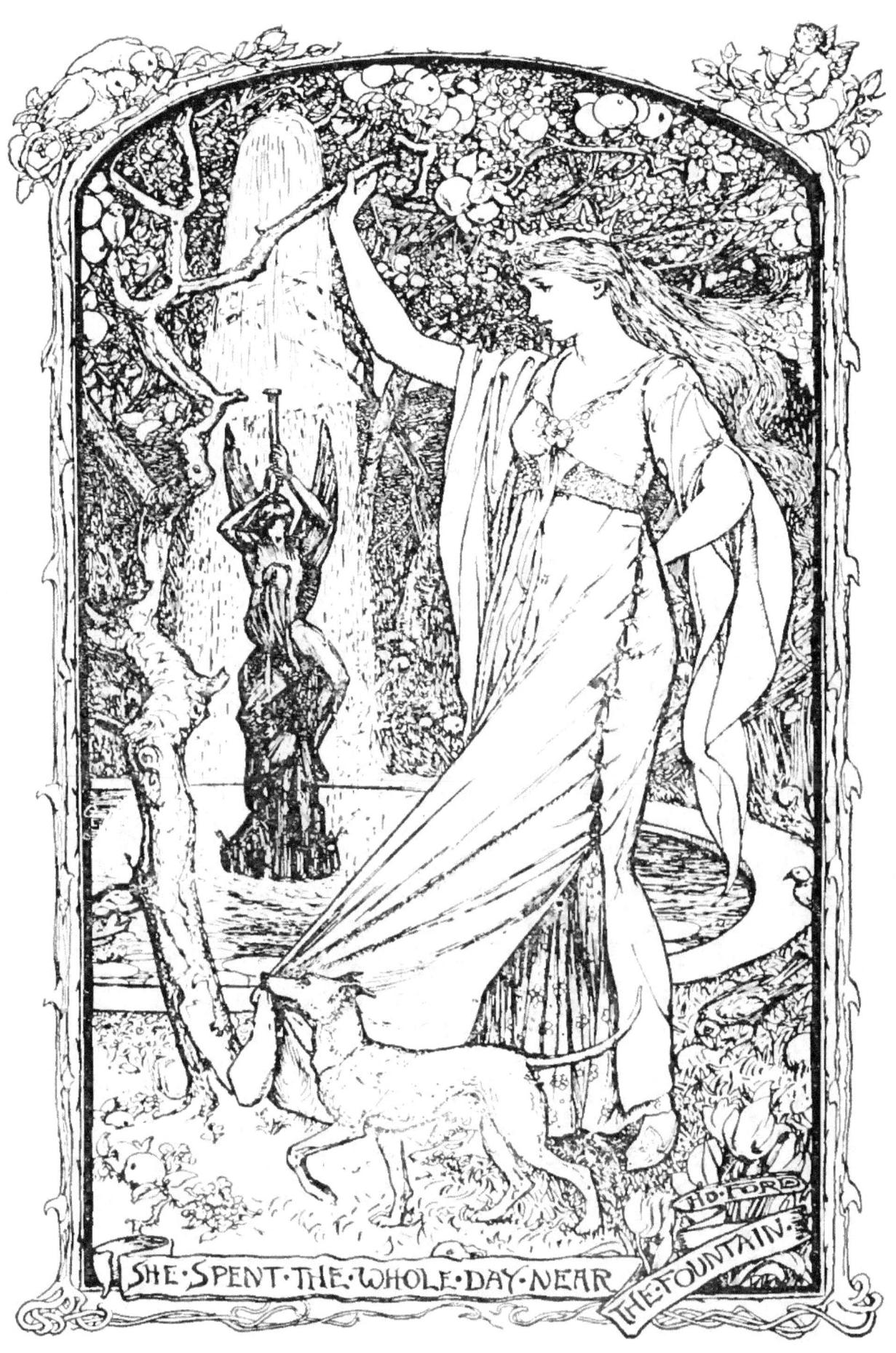
SHE SPENT THE WHOLE DAY NEAR THE FOUNTAIN

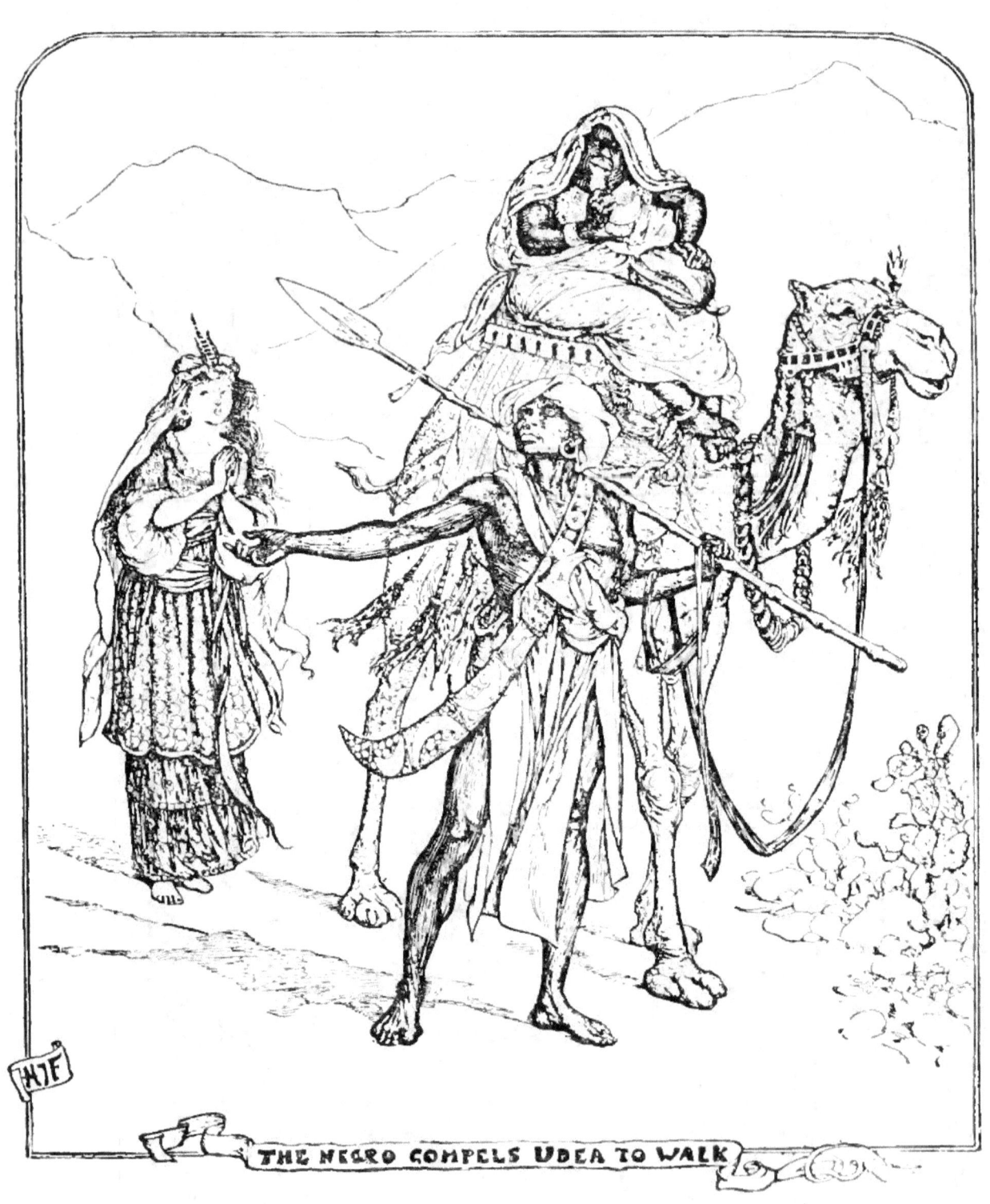
THE NEGRO COMPELS UBEA TO WALK

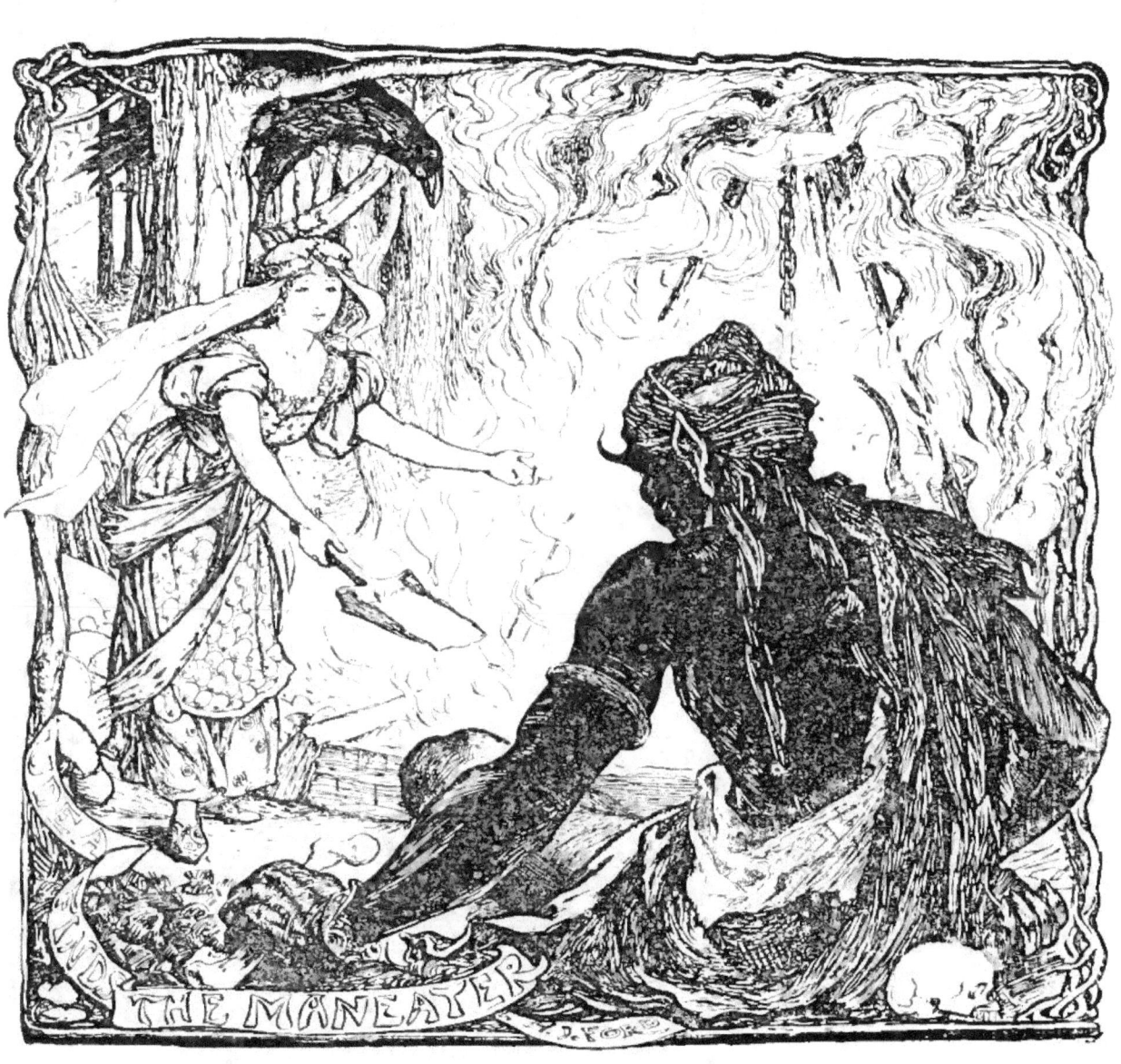

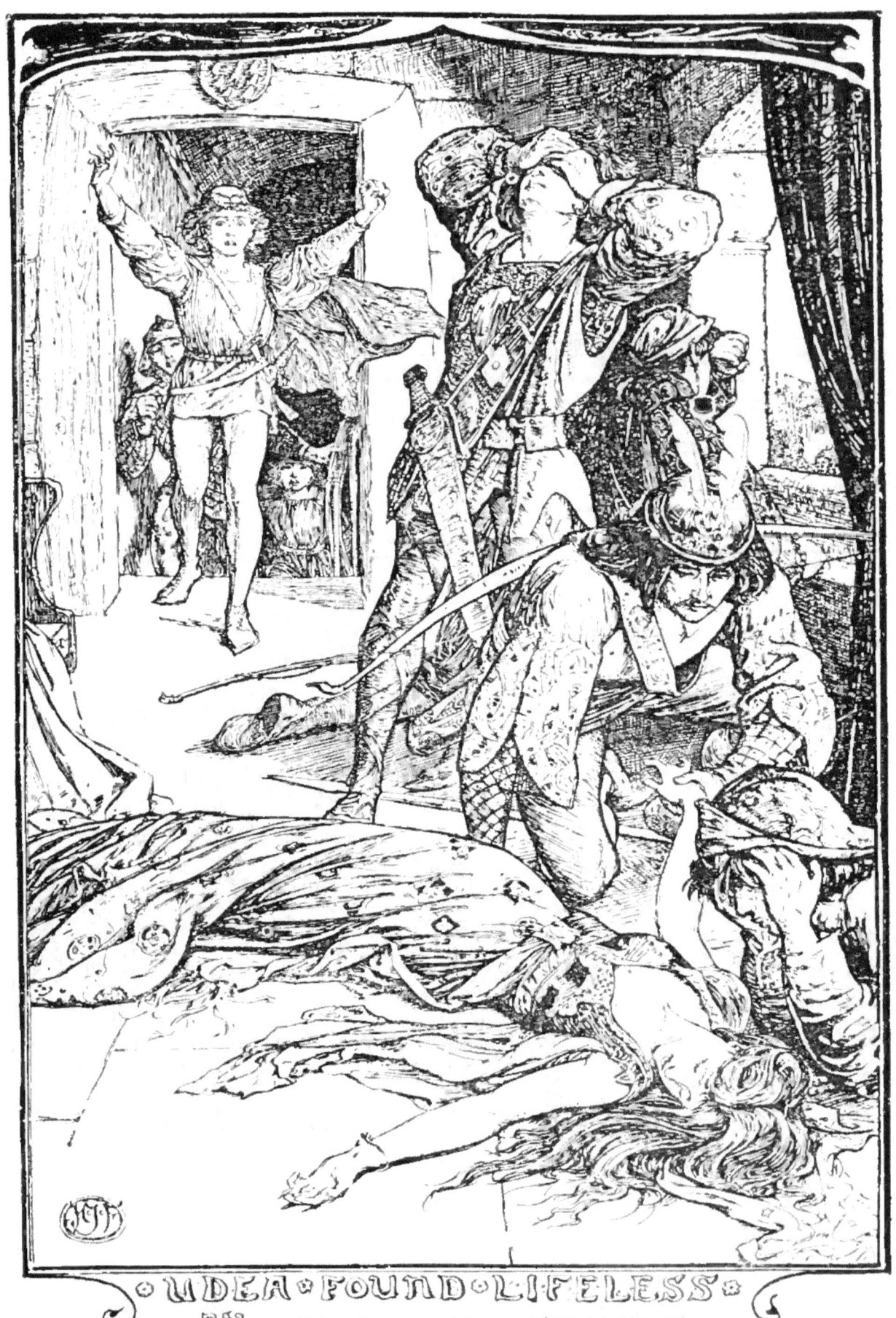

Udea found lifeless by her seven brothers

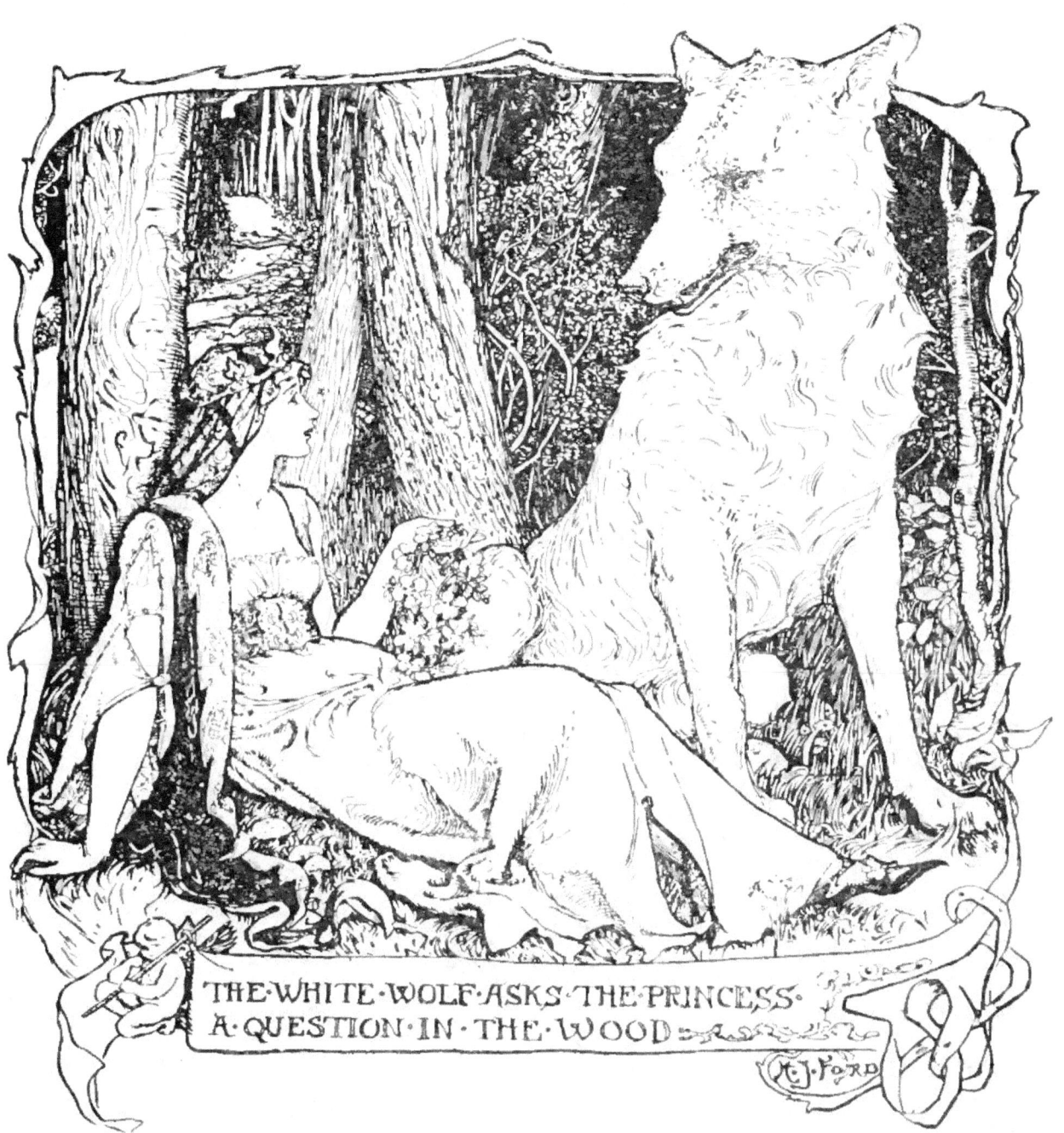
THE WHITE WOLF ASKS THE PRINCESS A QUESTION IN THE WOOD

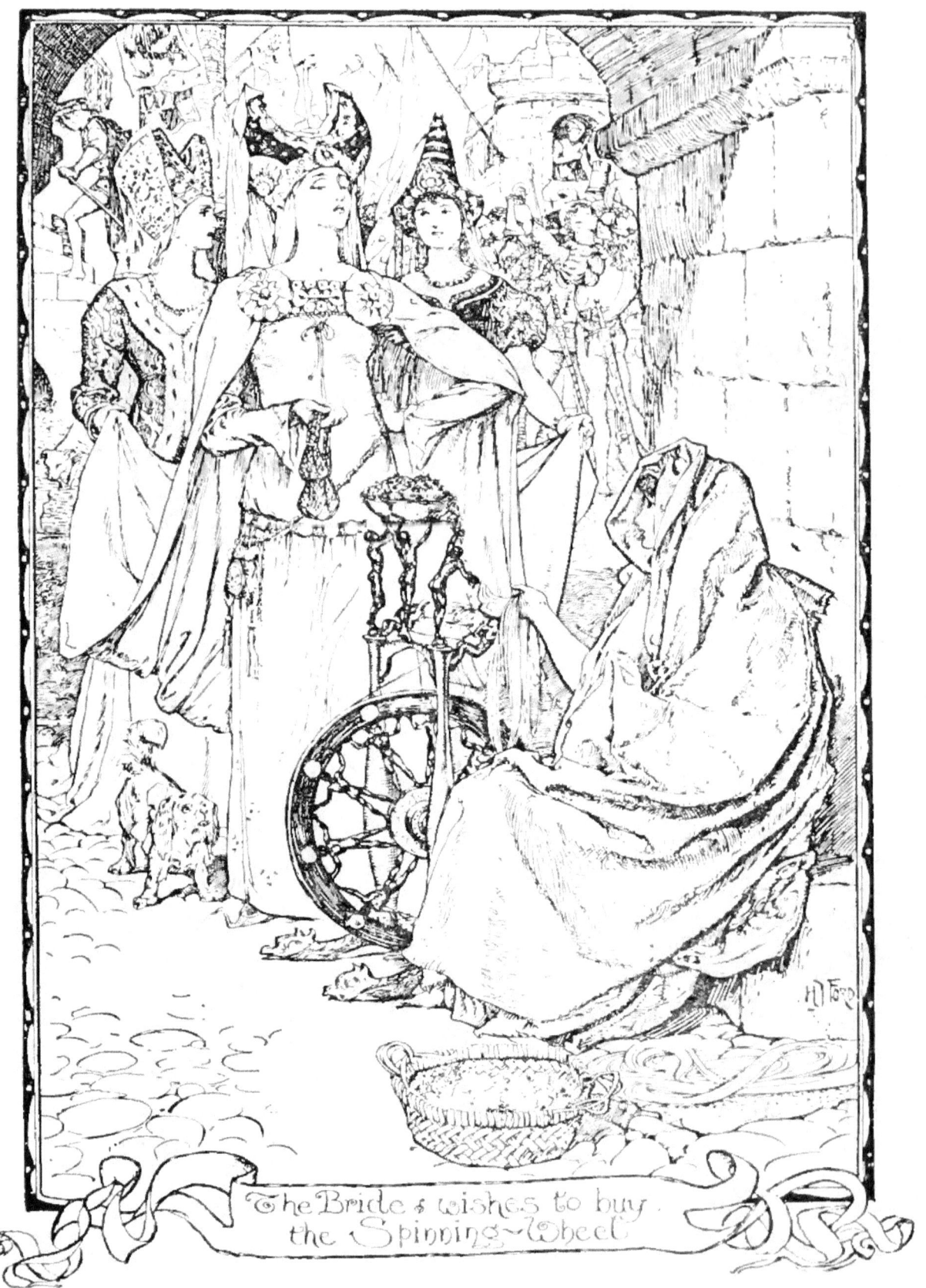

The Bride wishes to buy the Spinning-Wheel

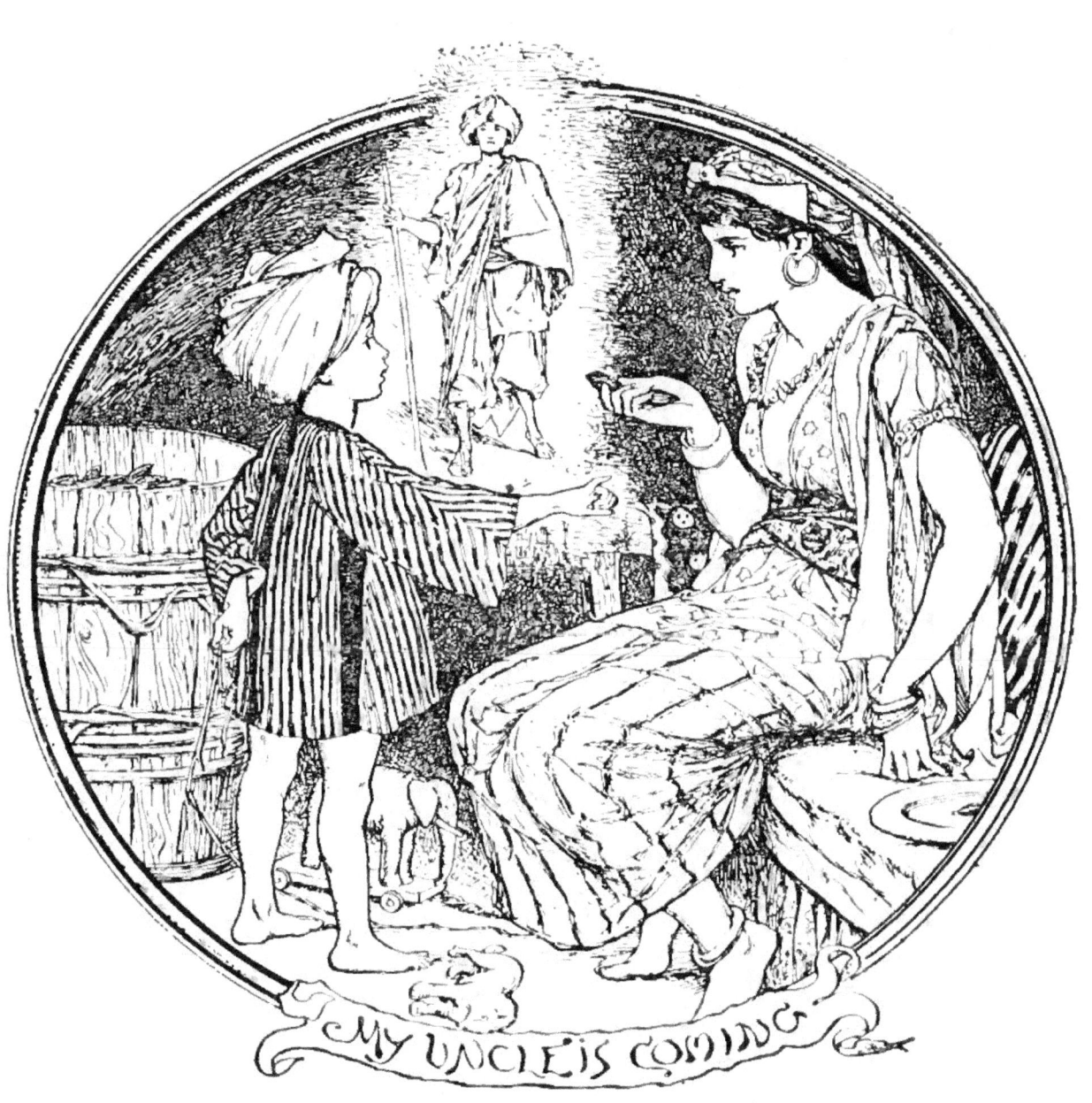

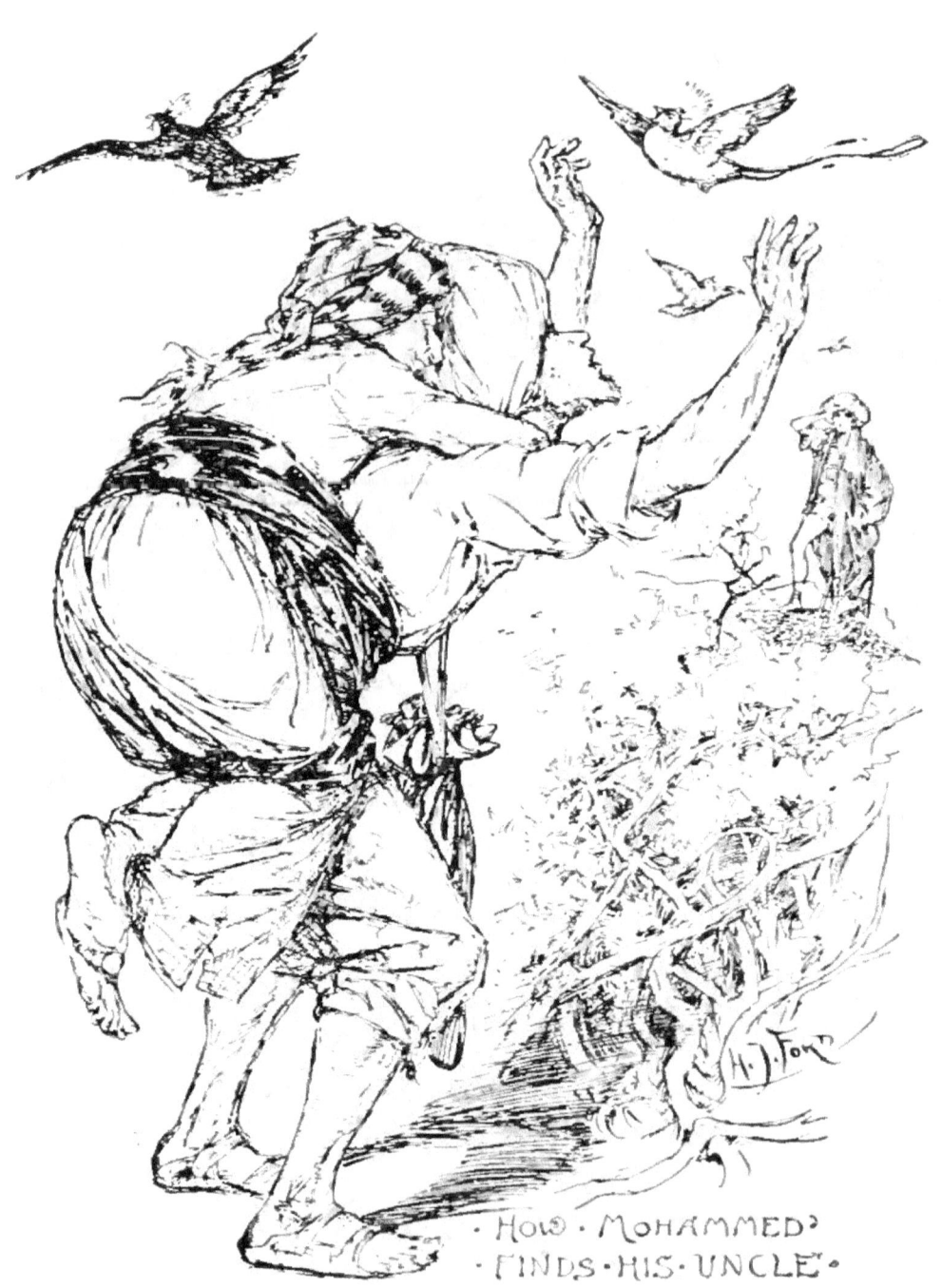
HOW MOHAMMED FINDS HIS UNCLE

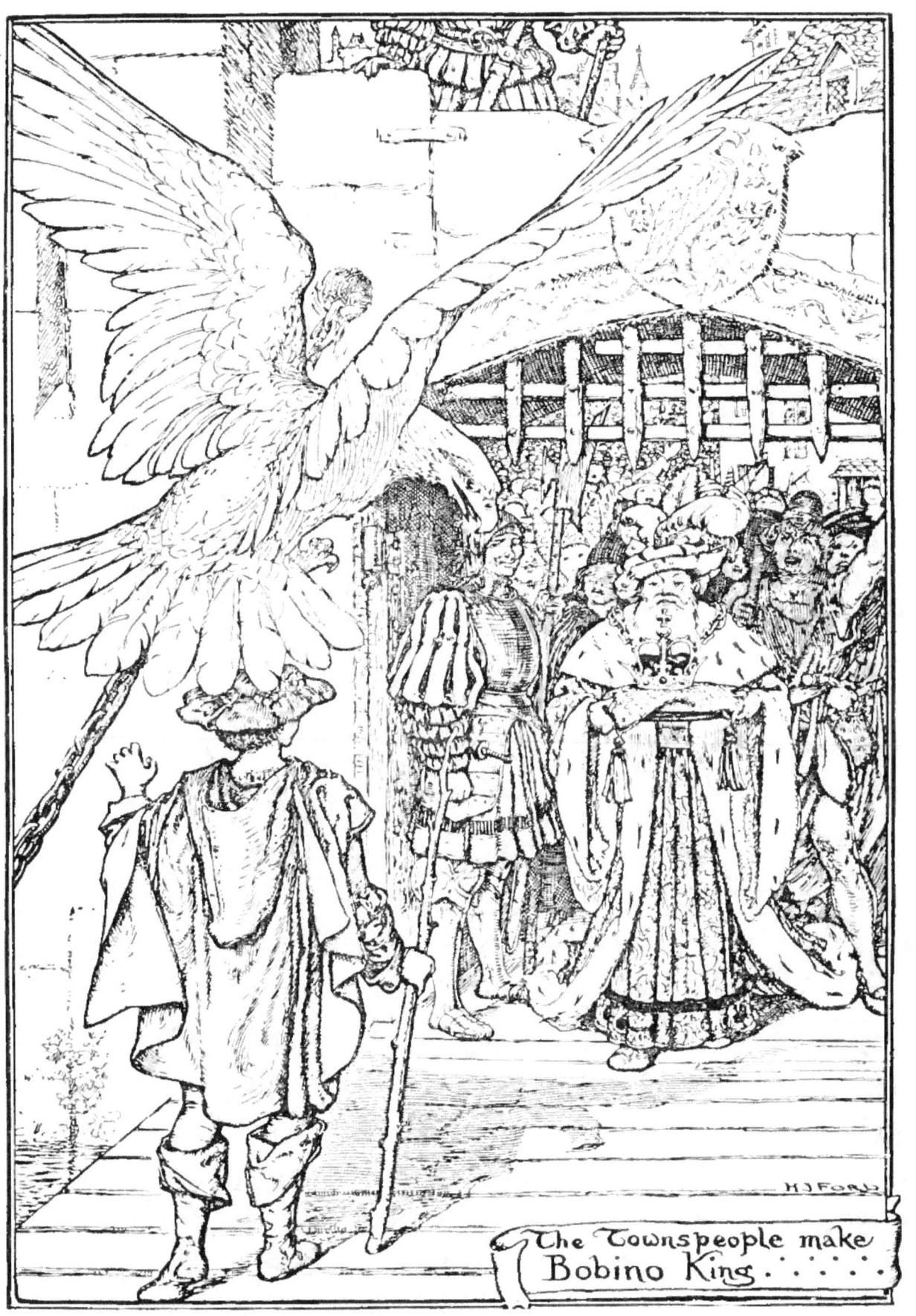
The Townspeople make Bobino King

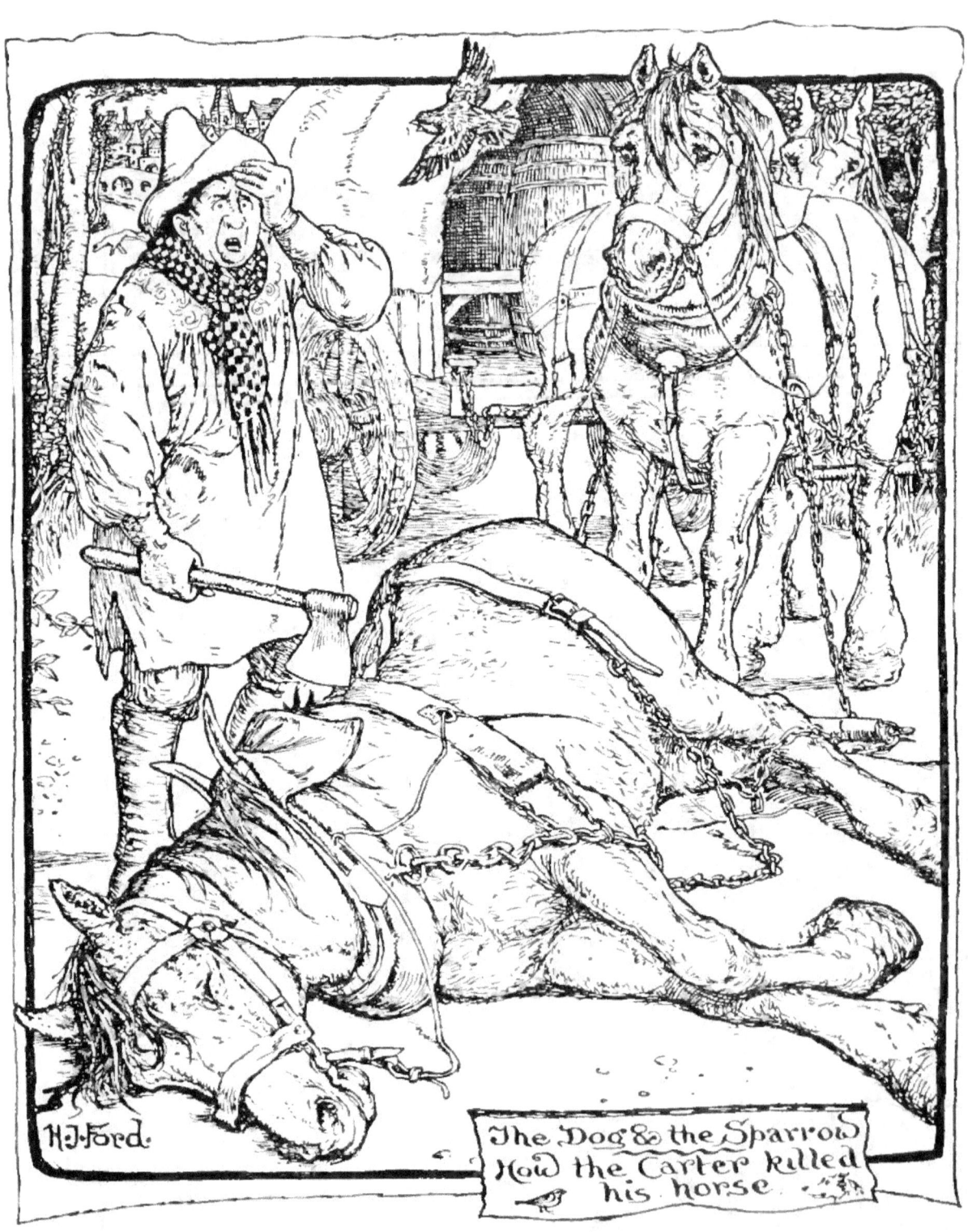
The Dog & the Sparrow
How the Carter killed his horse

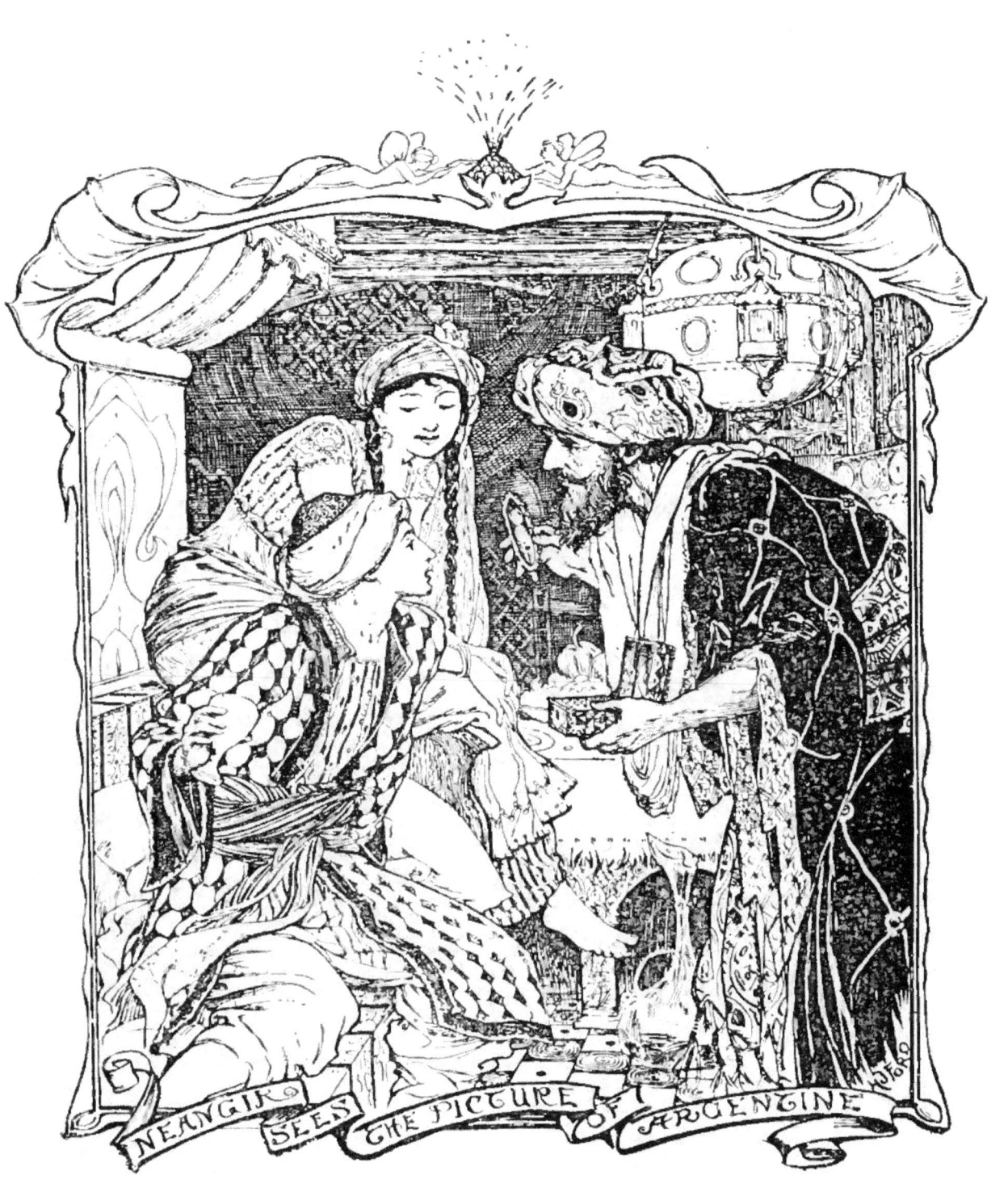

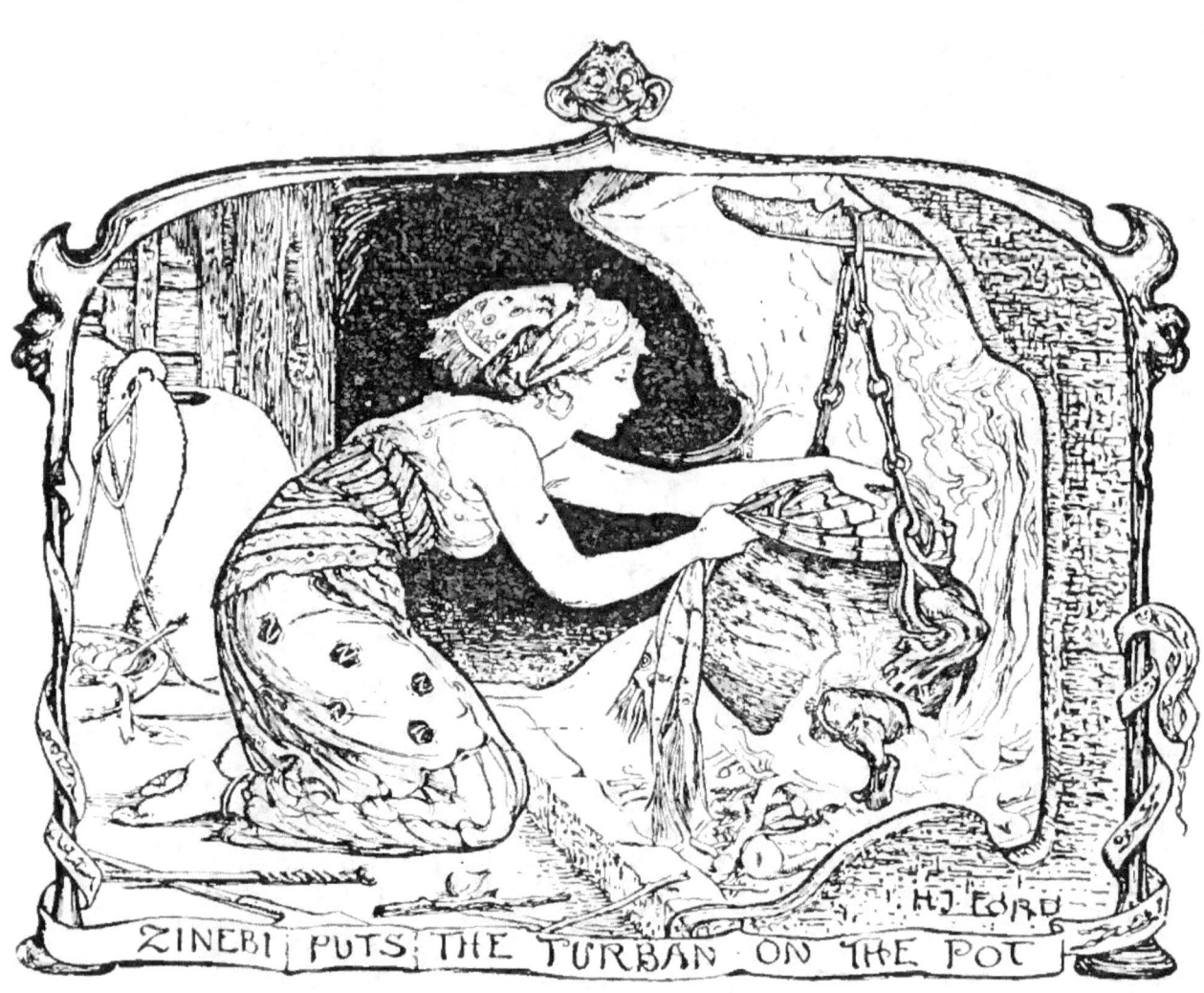

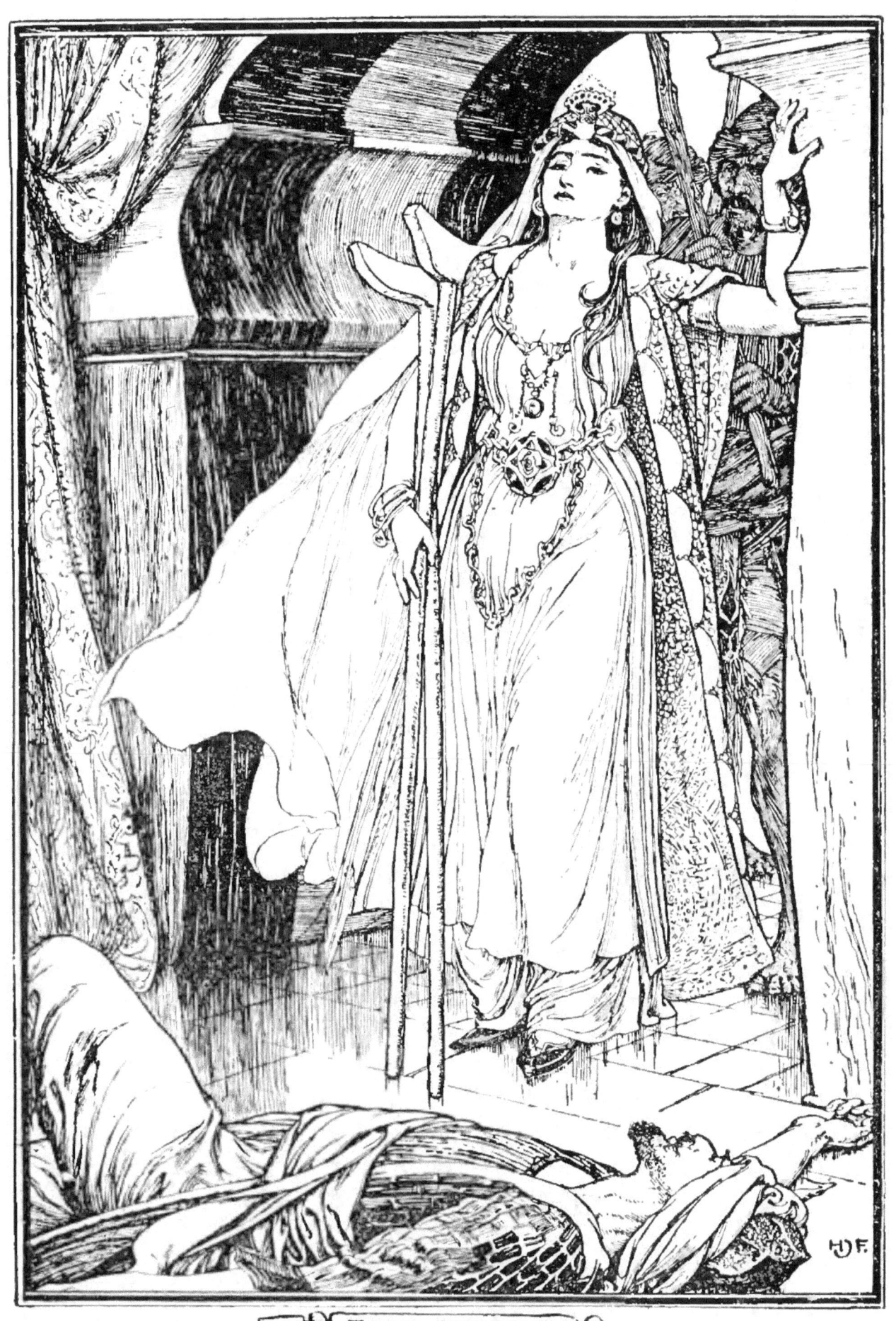

THERE APPEARED IN THE DOORWAY A LOVELY JEWESS

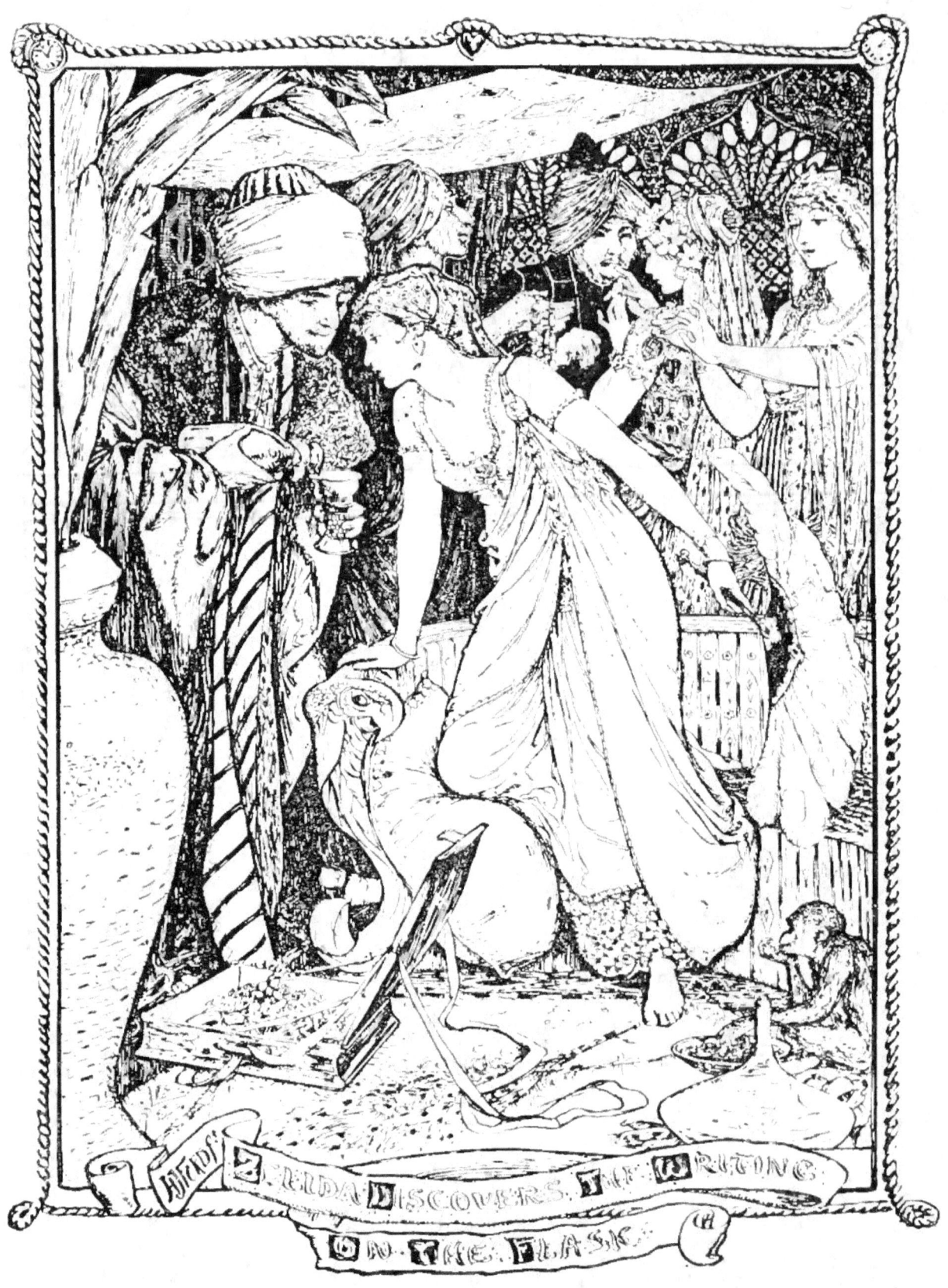

Zaida discovers the writing on the flask

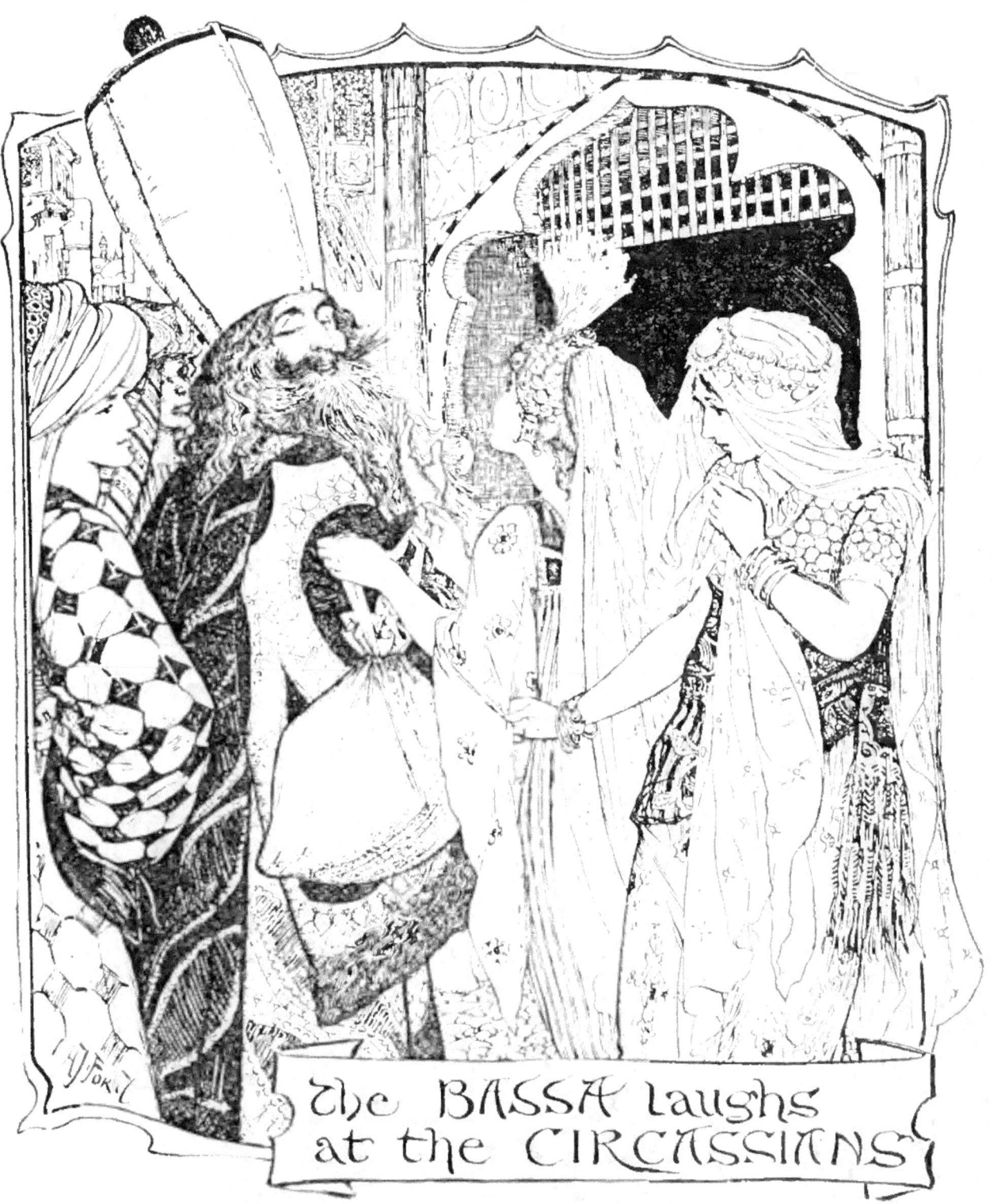
The BASSA laughs at the CIRCASSIANS

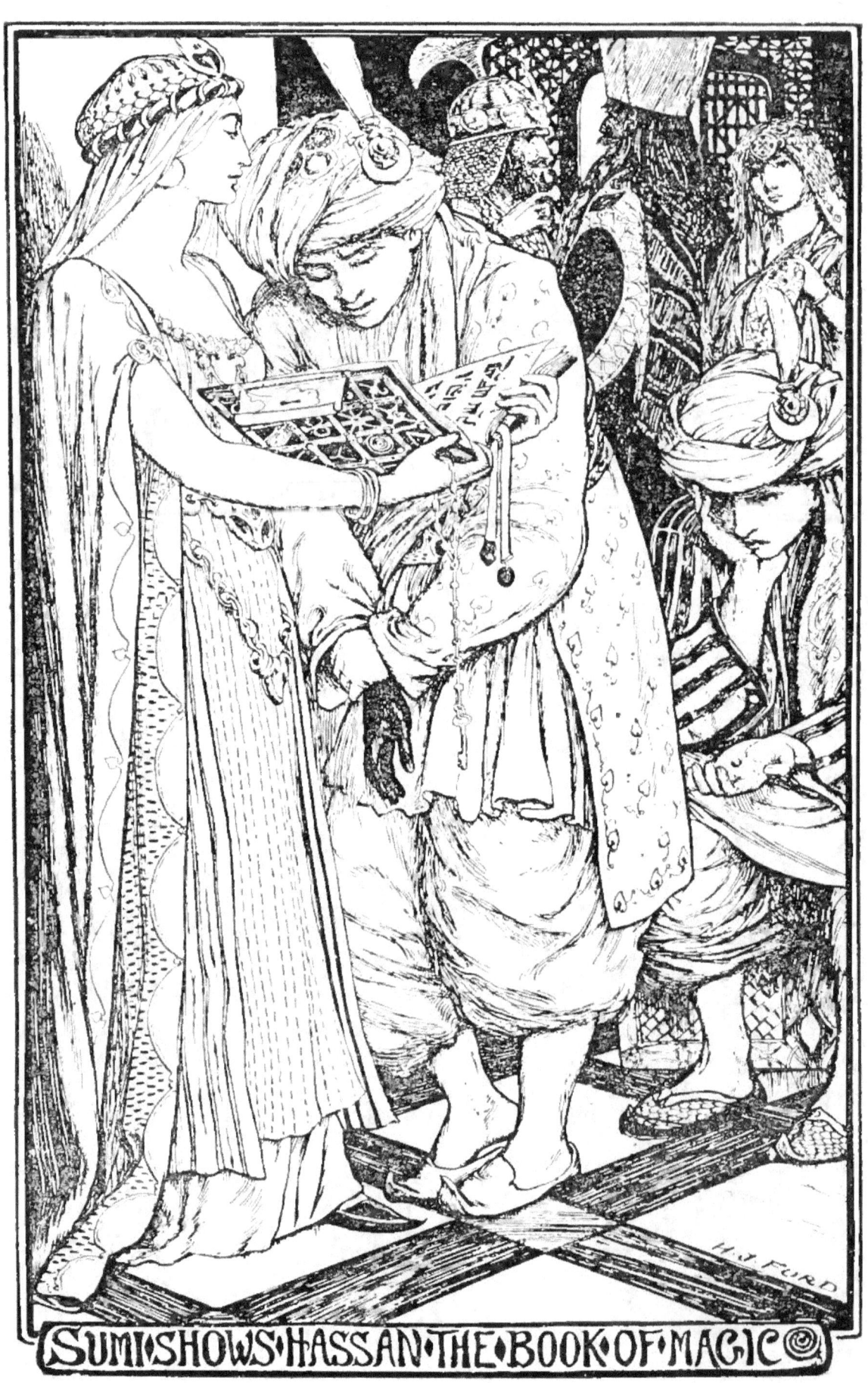

SUMI SHOWS HASSAN THE BOOK OF MAGIC

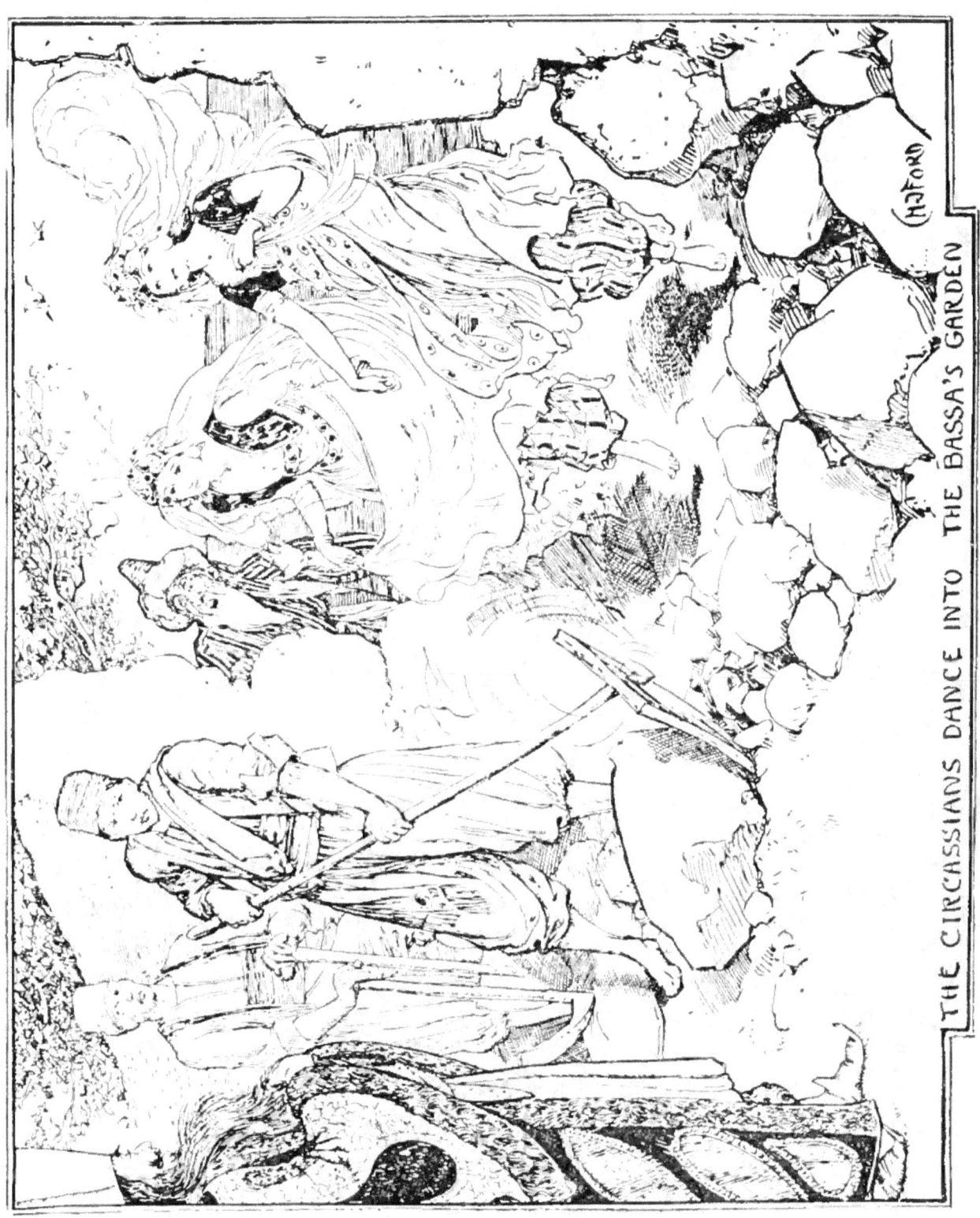

THE CIRCASSIANS DANCE INTO THE BASSA'S GARDEN

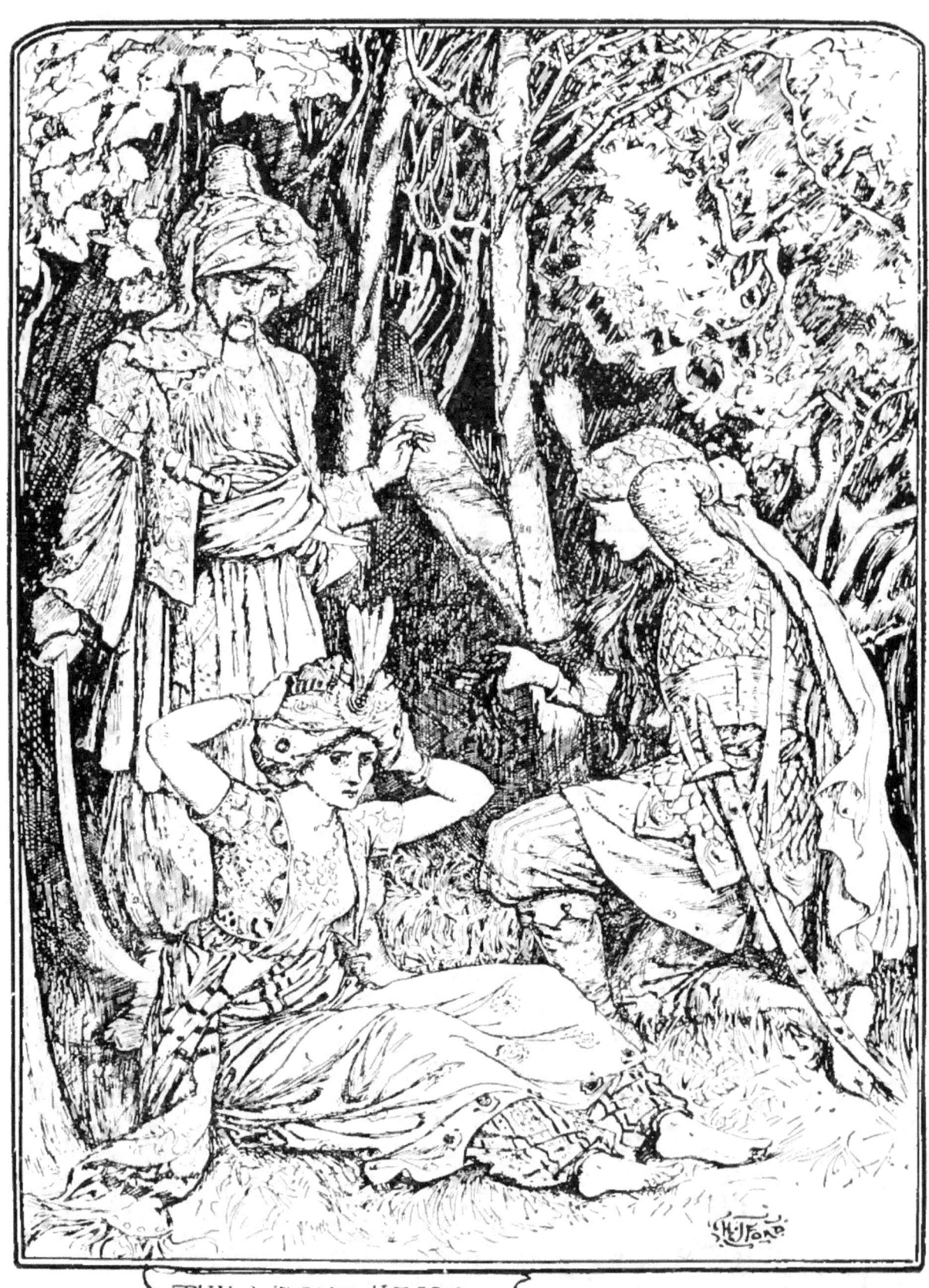

THE WRONG HEADS ON THE WRONG BODIES

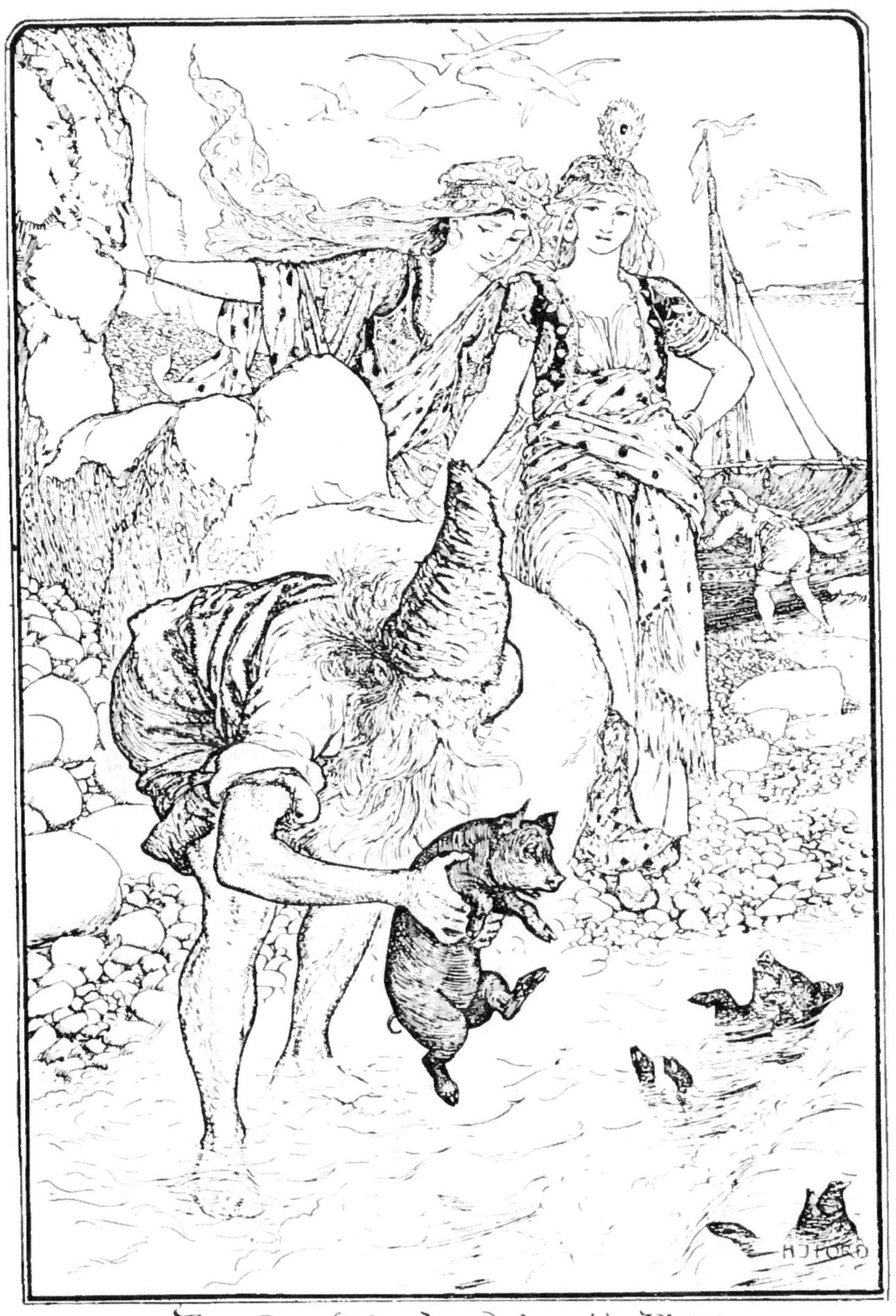

The Dervish drowning the Pigs

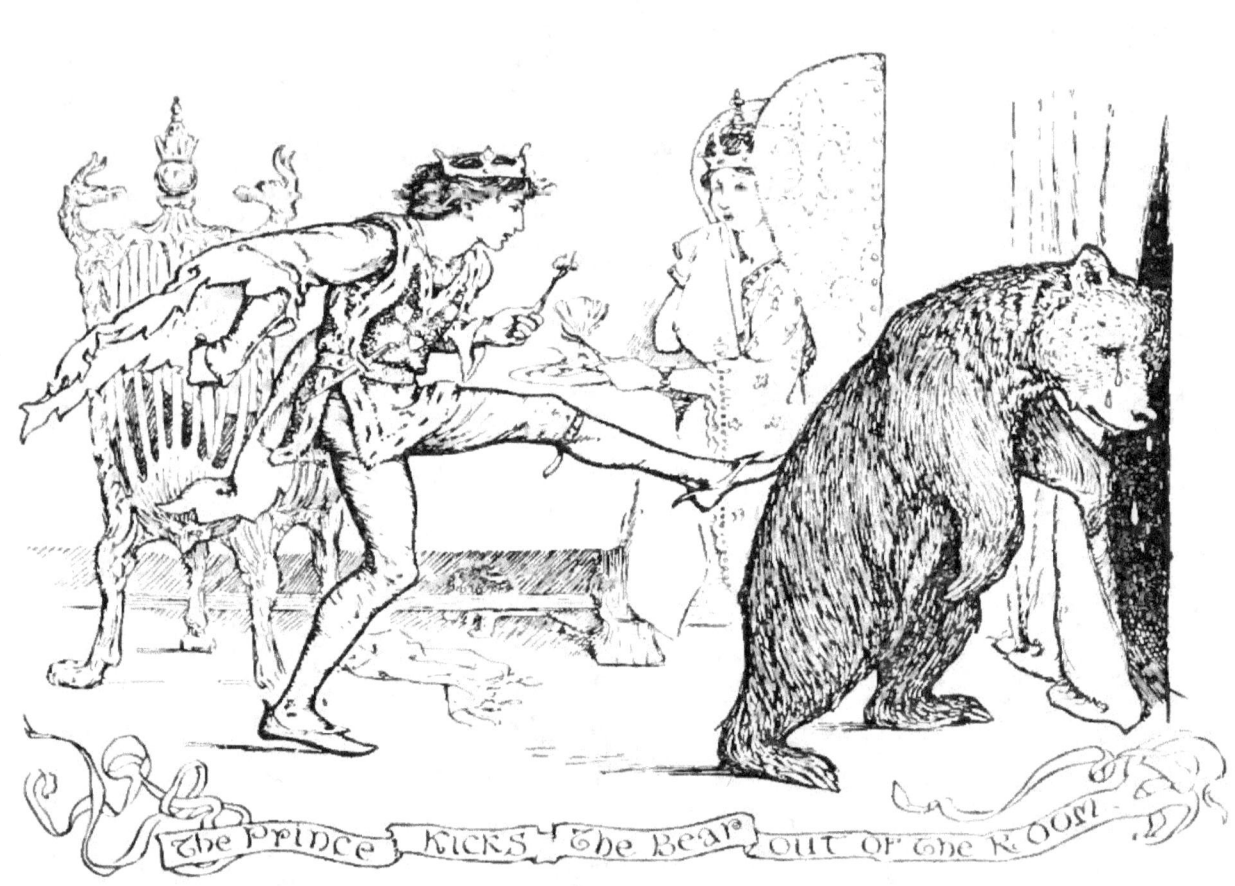
The Prince kicks the Bear out of the Room

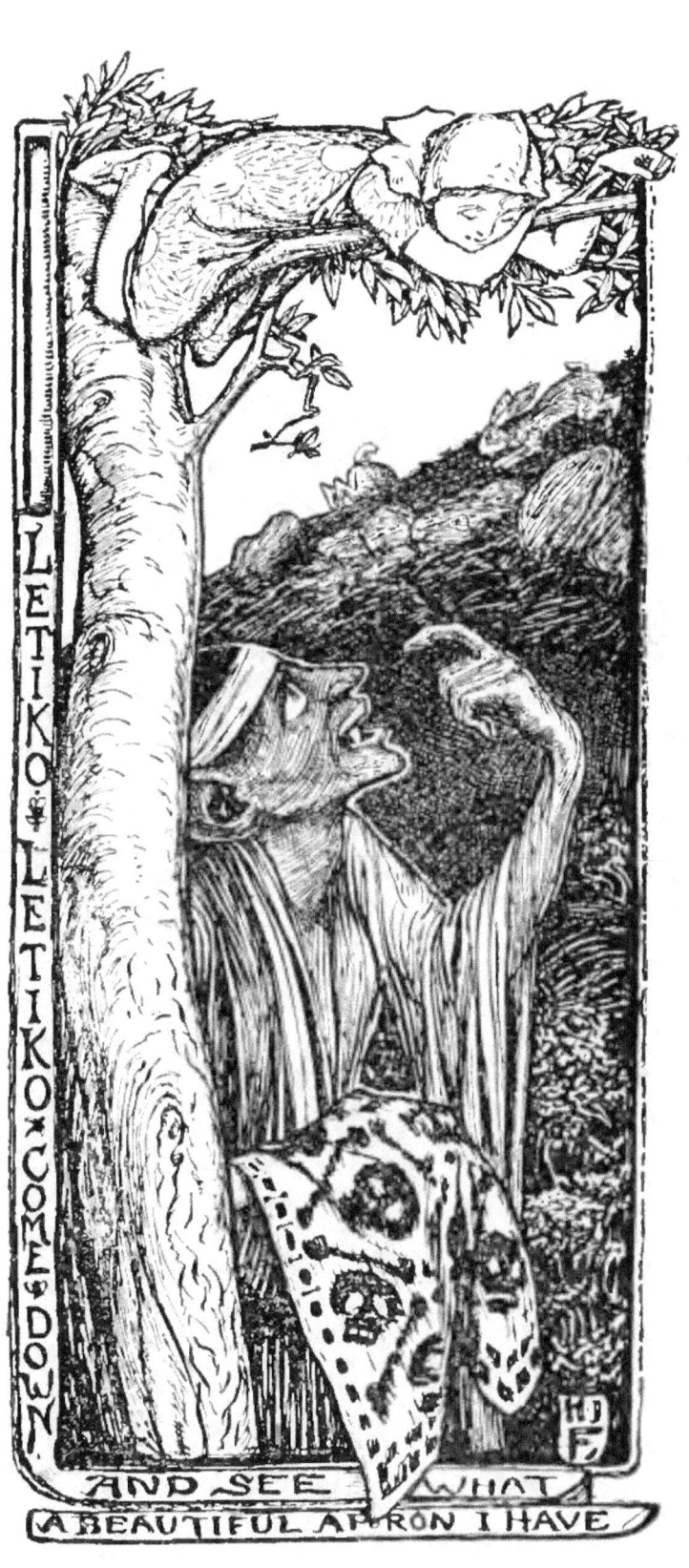

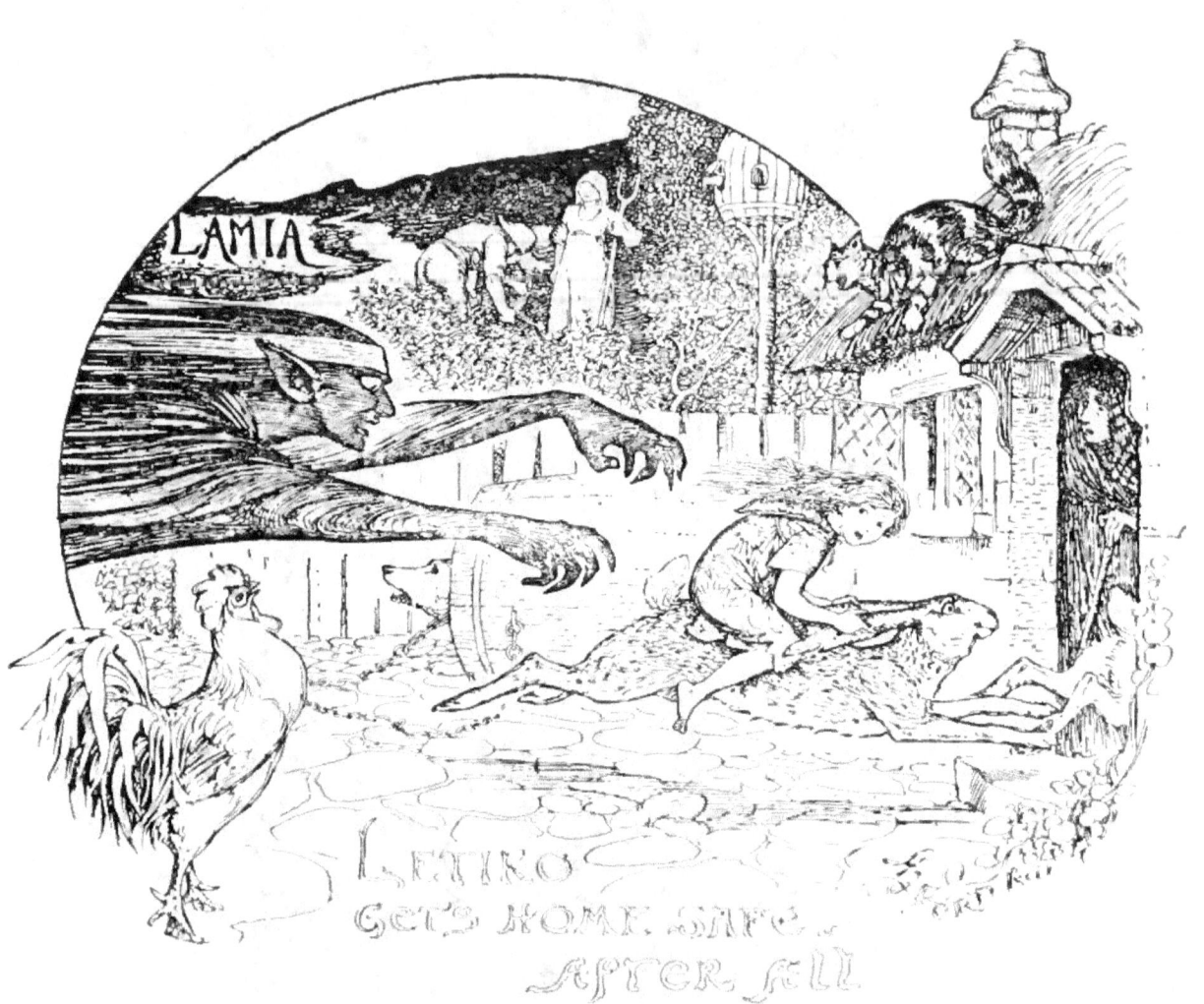

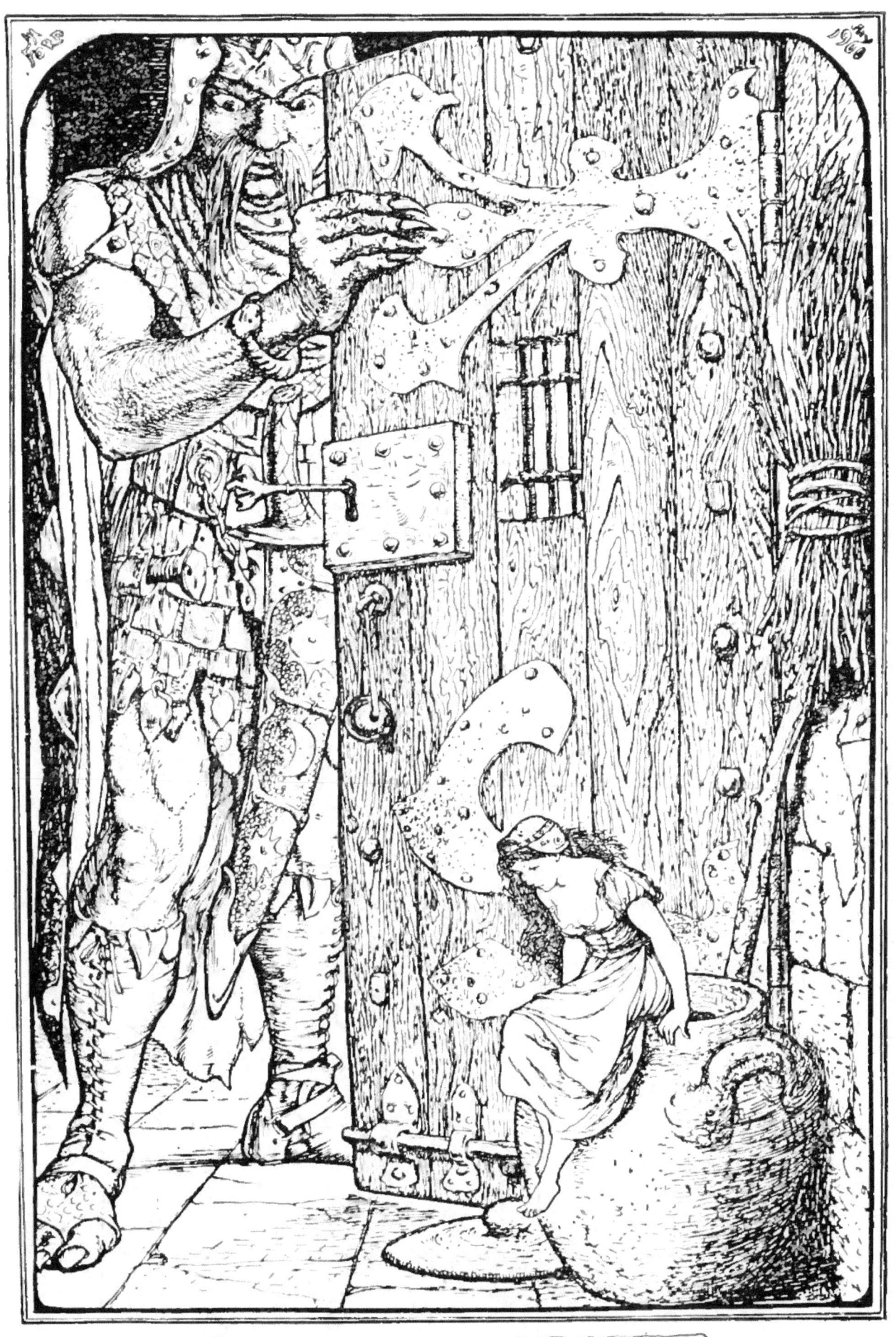

The Maiden creeps out of the Pot.

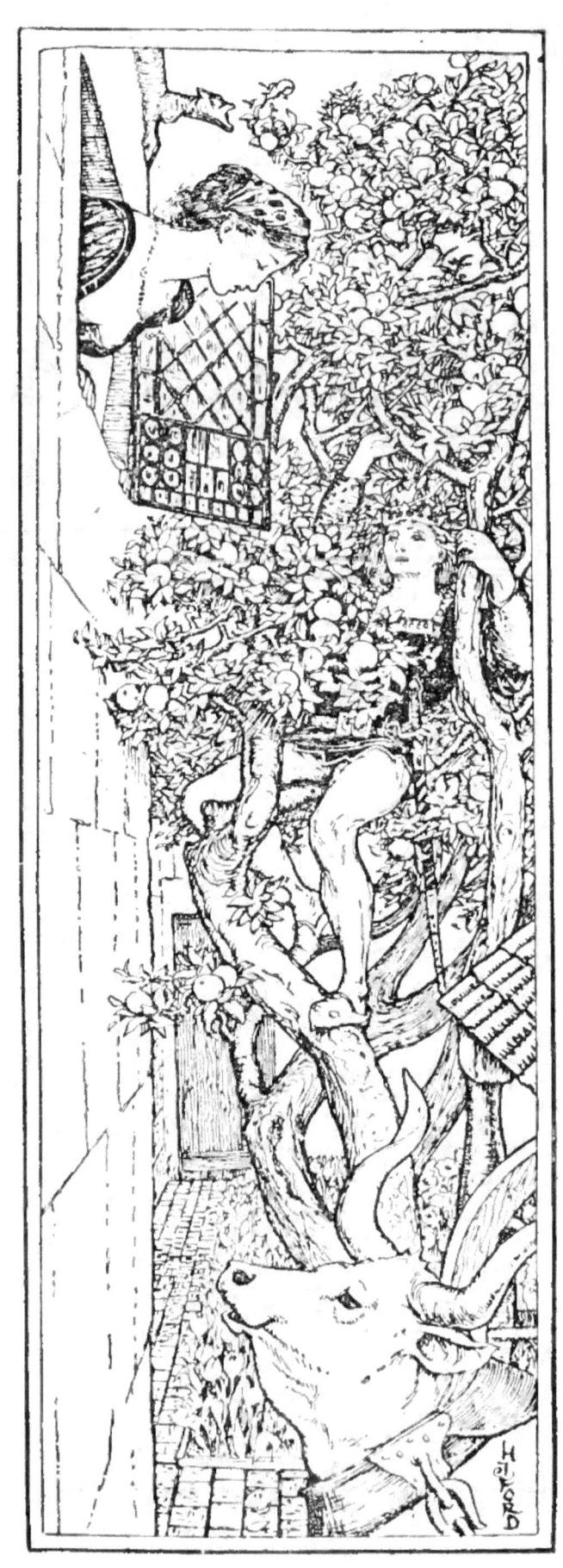

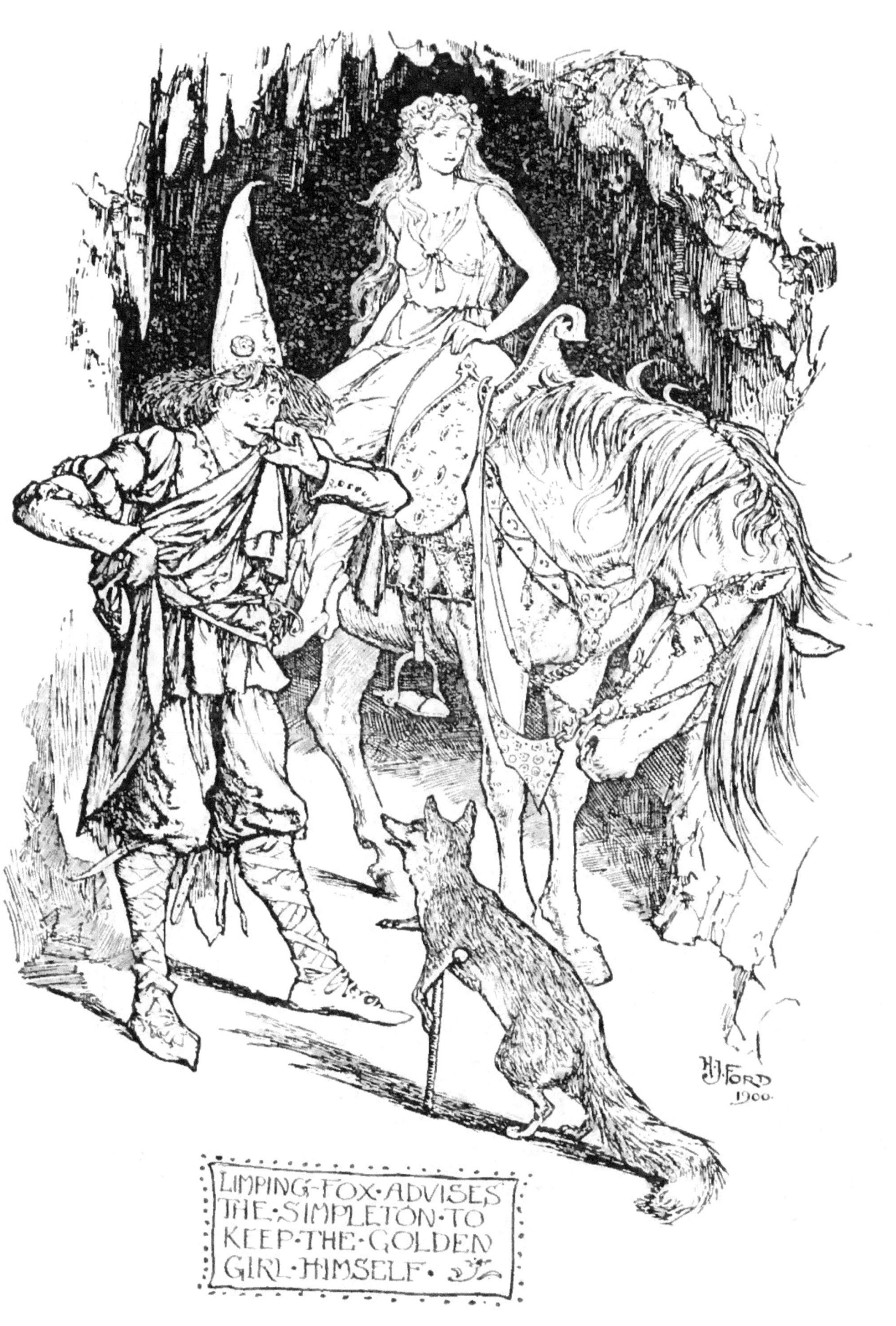

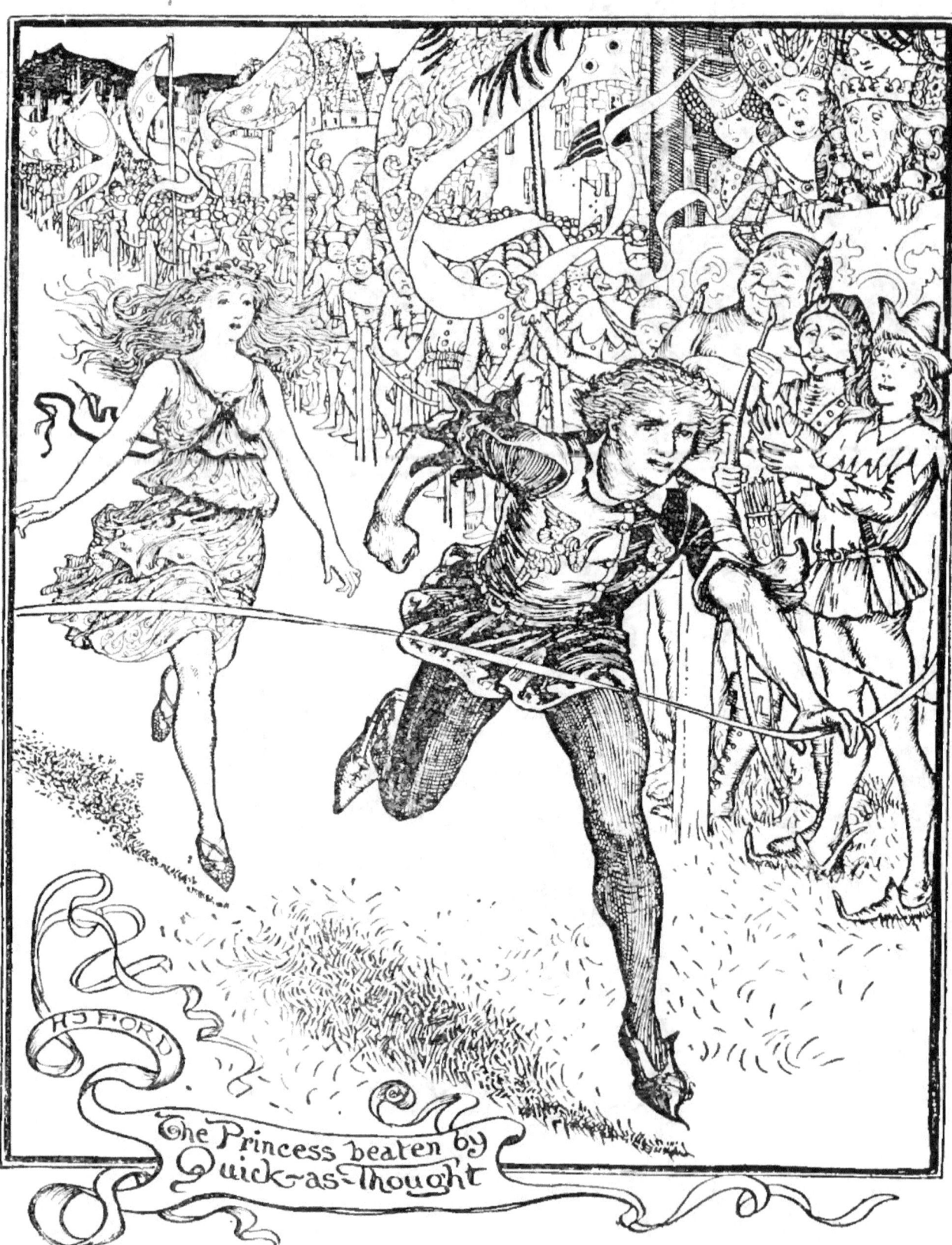

The Princess beaten by Quick-as-Thought

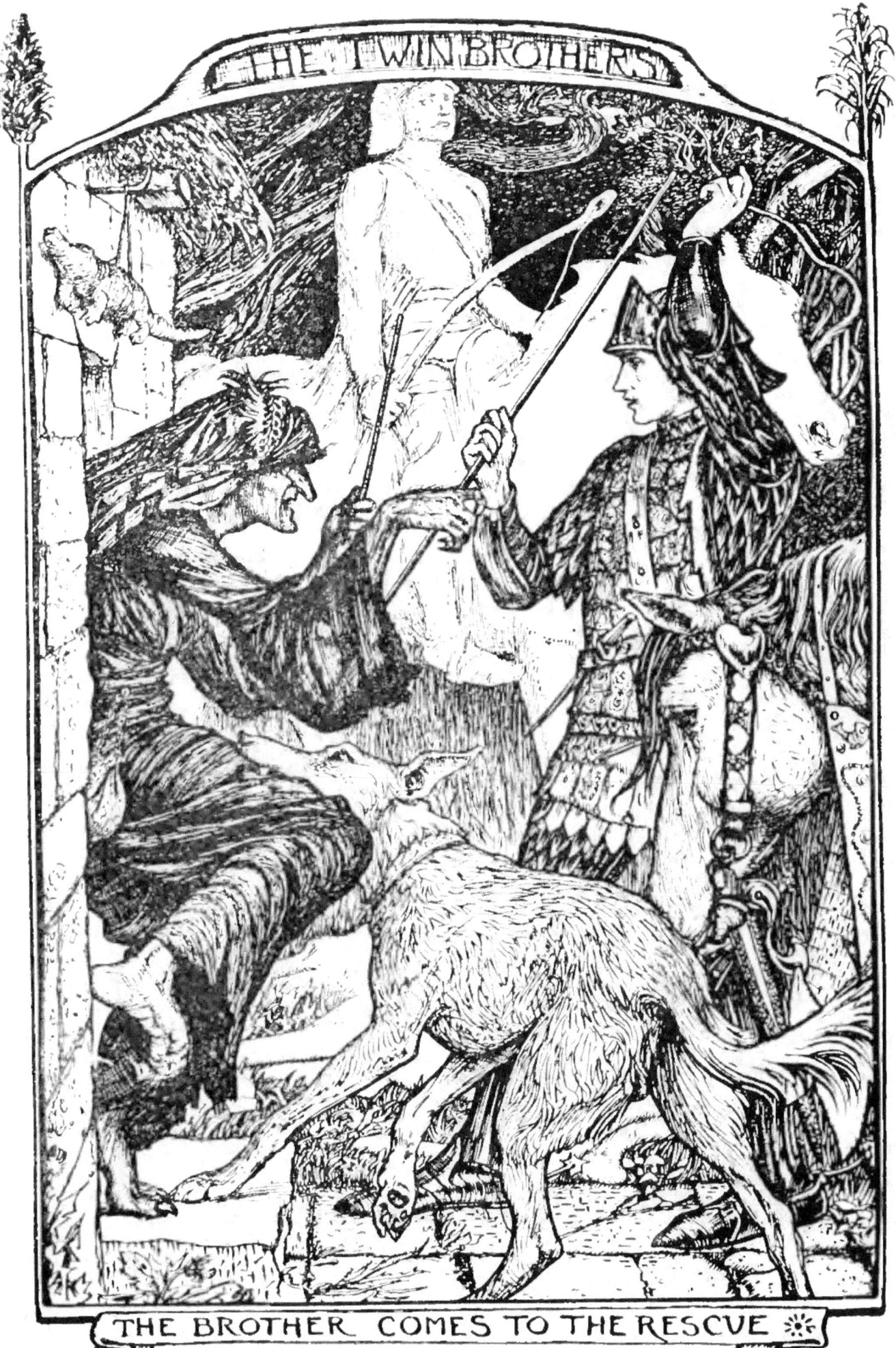

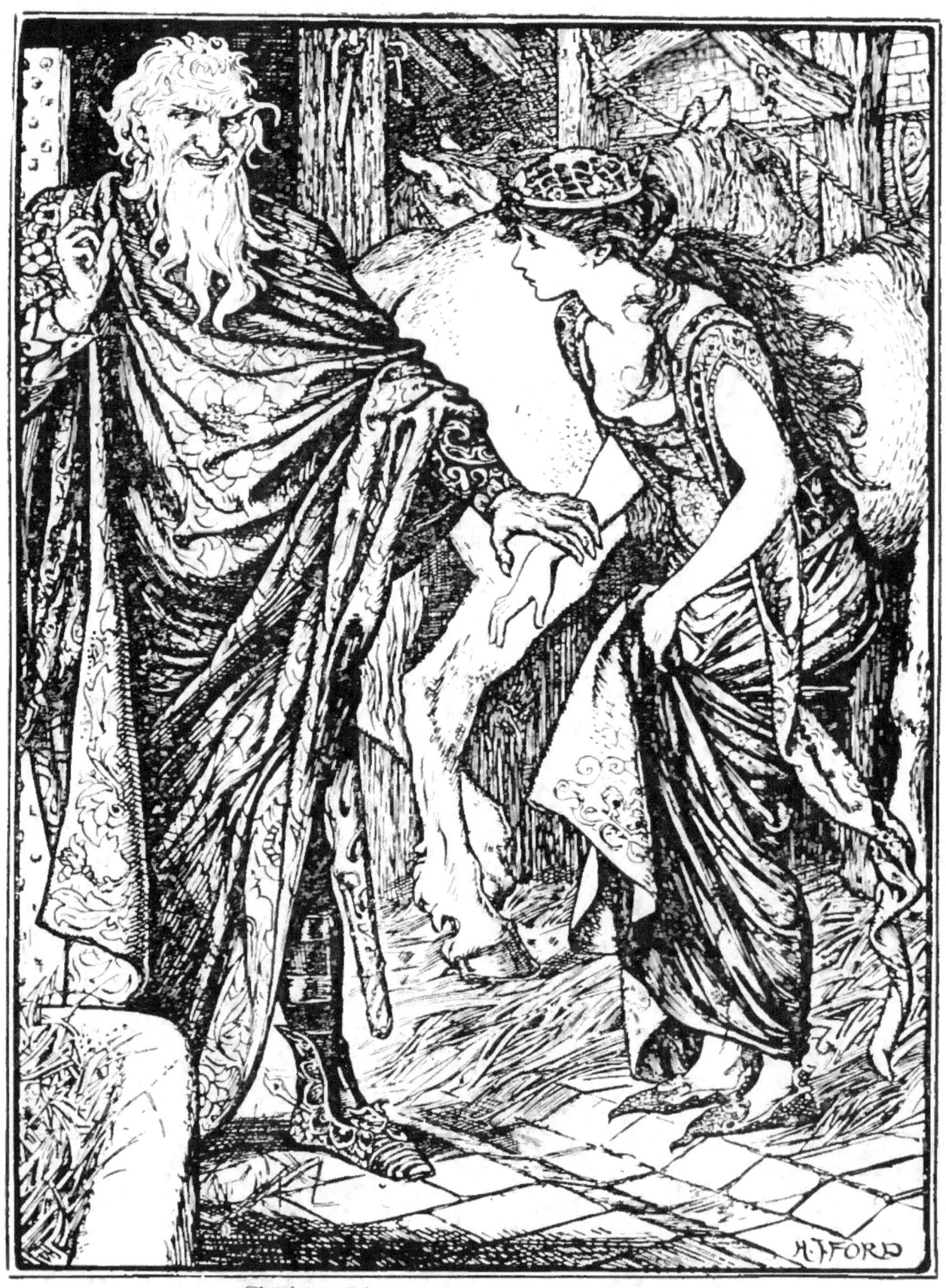

SCIORAVANTE LEAVES CANNETELLA IN THE STABLE

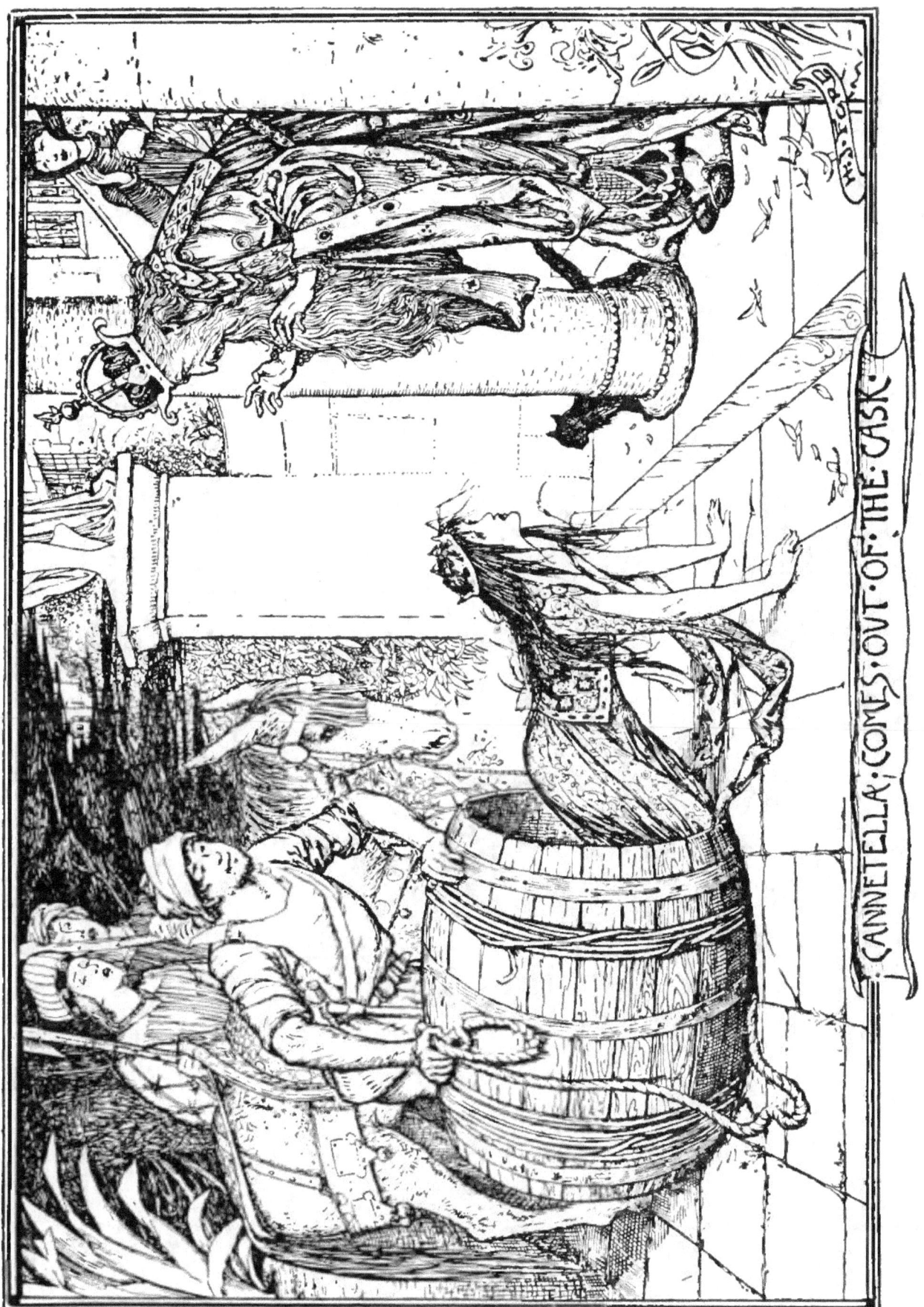

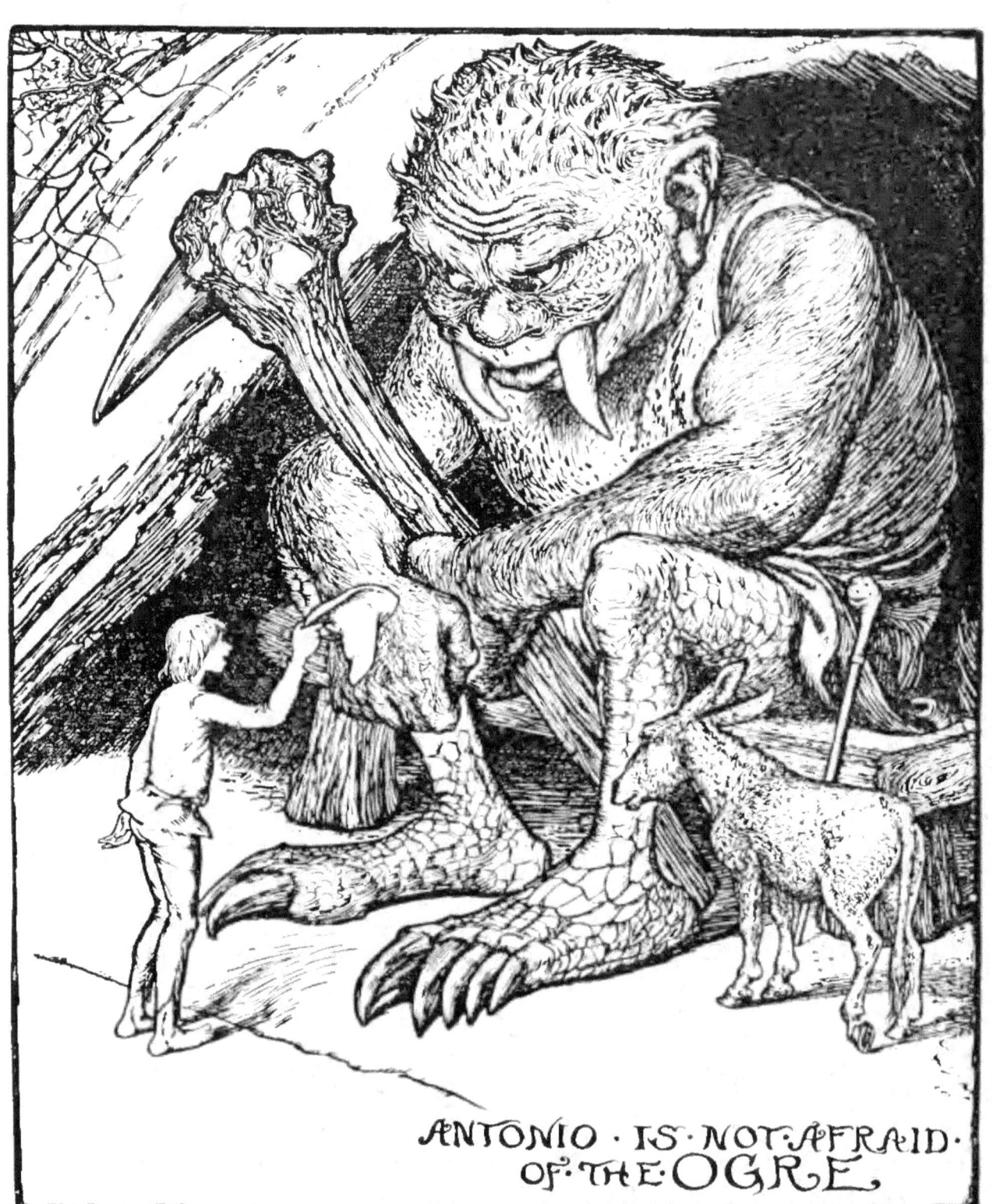

ANTONIO IS NOT AFRAID OF THE OGRE.

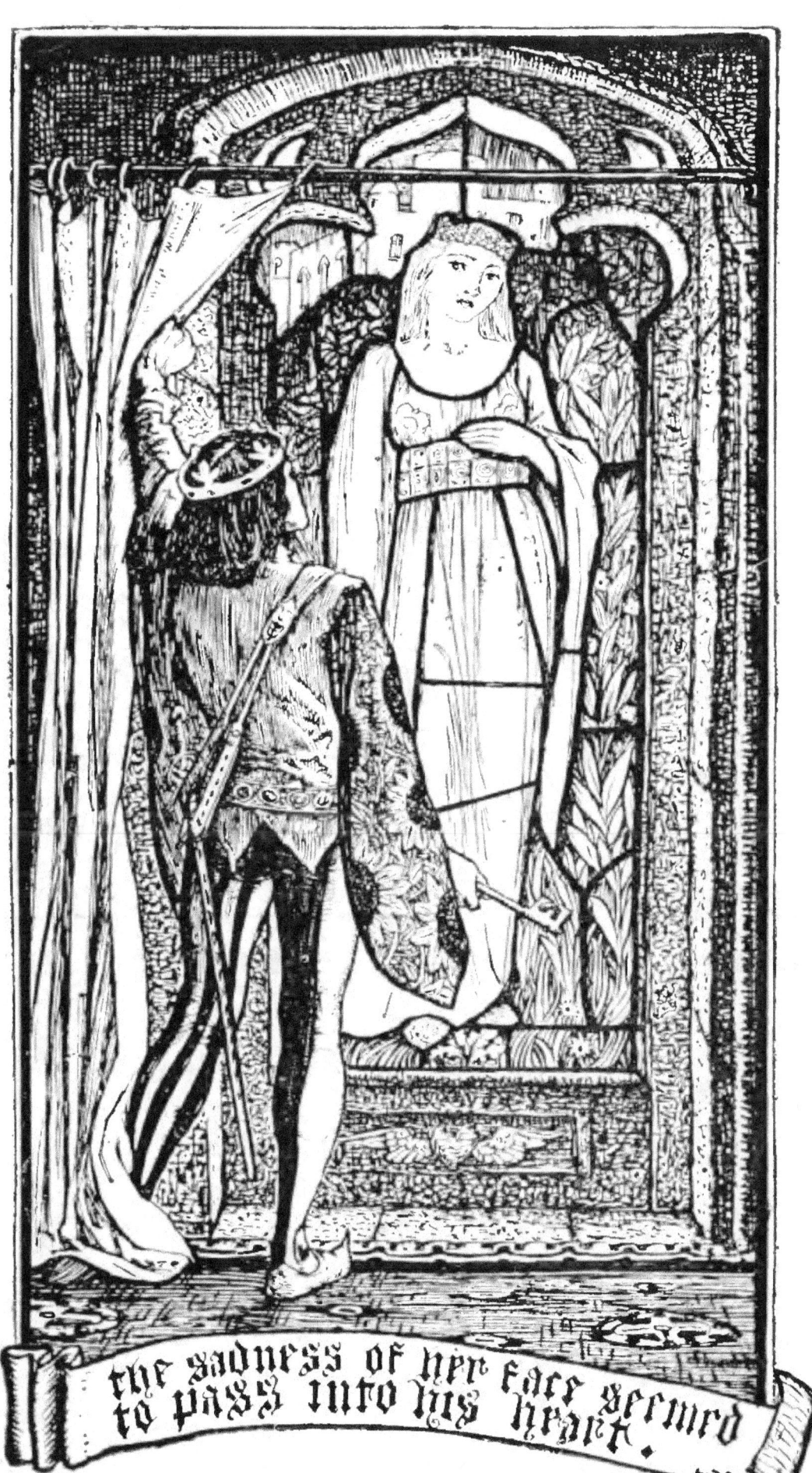

the sadness of her face seemed to pass into his heart.

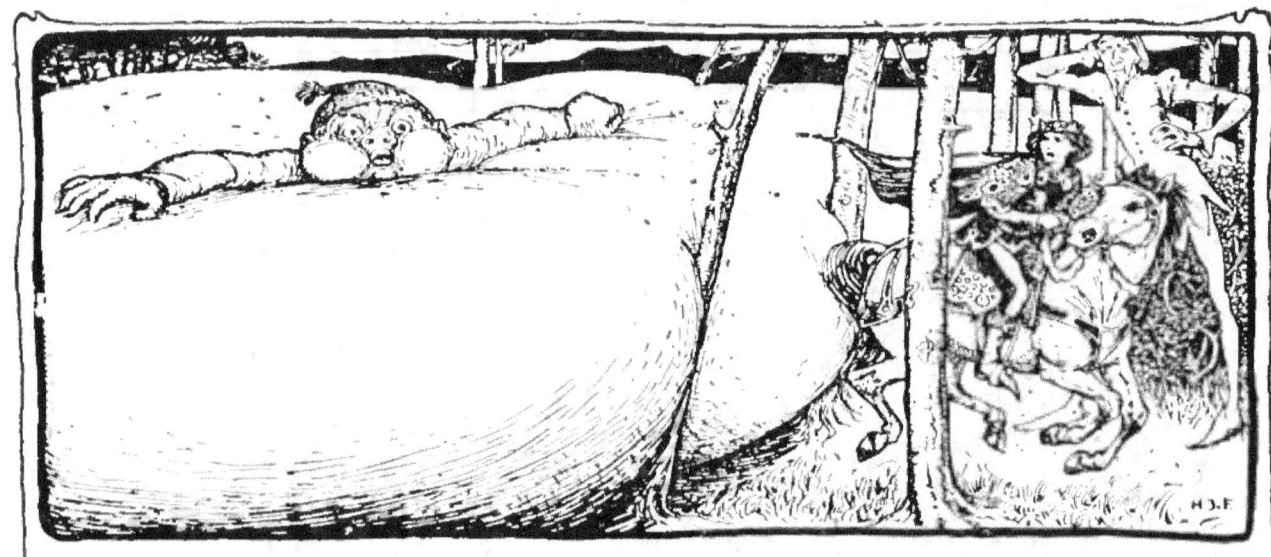

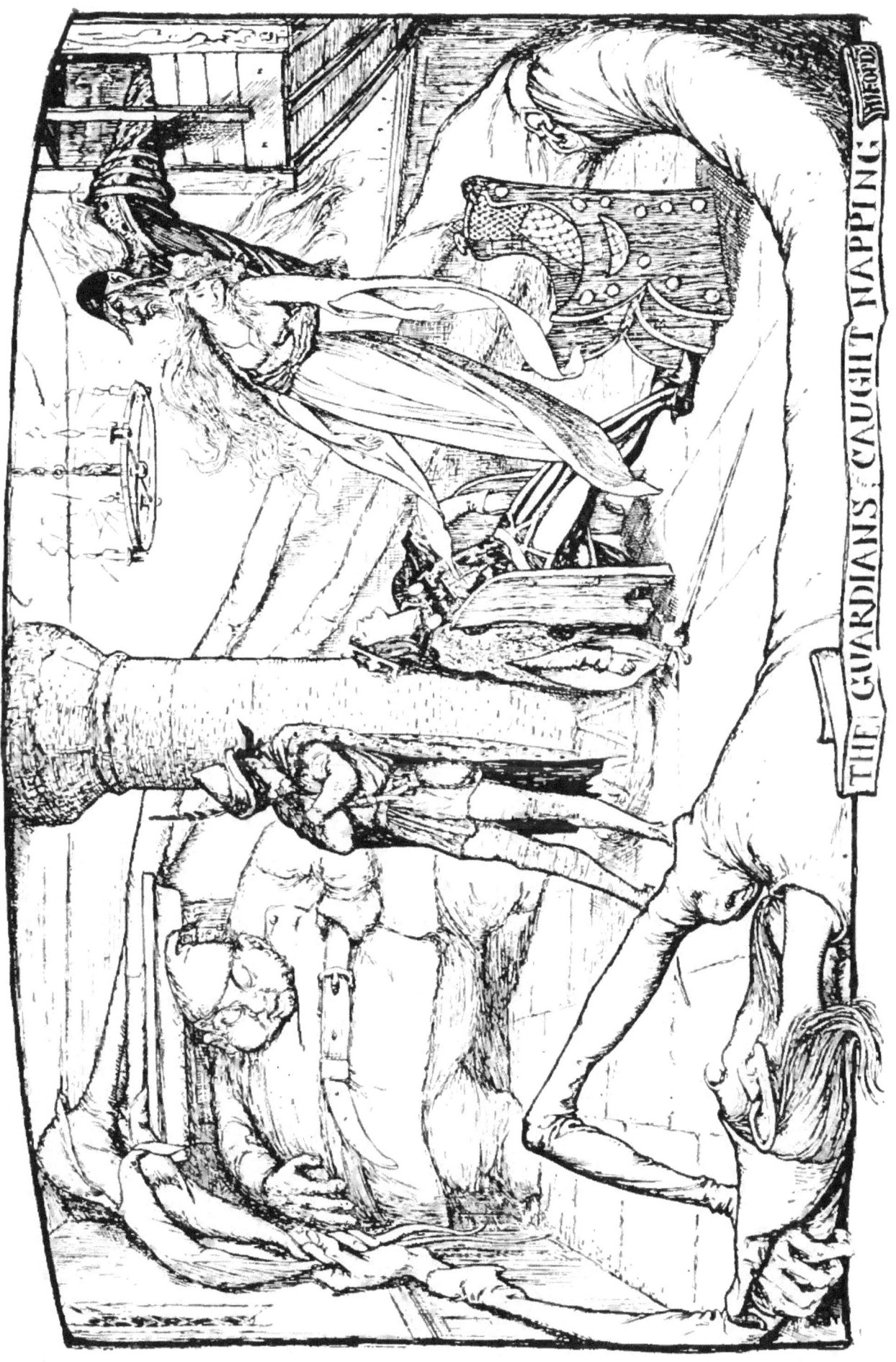
THE GUARDIANS CAUGHT NAPPING